Unspeakable Joy

Kristi Coen

May these words of my mouth and this meditation of my heart be pleasing in your sight, Lord, my Rock and my Redeemer.

Psalm 19:14

CONTENTS

A note from the editor:

Beginning on page 111 of this book Kristi has shared some pictures of Sydnee at different stages of her life. Kristi felt that sharing these pictures would help her readers to better understand the challenges that Sydnee faced.

Sydnee's parents do not look at their daughter and see her birth defects. They see her beautiful smile and spirit. The deformations do not define Sydnee as a person in their eyes. Because of their example Sydnee did not feel sorry for herself. She lived with the hand she was dealt as best she could—which was better than most.

-Jana Bontrager

Sydnee's Story

DEDICATION

For Scott. You have been my cheerleader, my encourager to keep writing when I wanted to give up so many times. You are my life, my love, my gift, and my very best friend.

For Kerri, my firstborn princess. You have a gift of compassion and a love for others.

For Sydnee, my second princess and now my treasure. I just knew God had great things in store for you. Now, I get the chance to share your story with others.

For Noah, my son. You are your own funny self, but you also have so many of Sydnee's mannerisms.

To any readers who have lost any child in your life. I pray that you will find comfort in this book, not because of me, but from God who comforts us so that we can comfort others. May you know that you are loved.

Chapter 1

SCOTT MEETS KRISTI

Scott and I met in September of 1998 after being set up by a pastor friend, Reverend Bret Layton. Reverend Layton explained that Scott was thinking of becoming a pediatrician or a pediatric oncologist. *Wow*, I thought, *this could work out! I love children and since I am hoping to work in the Neonatal Intensive Care Unit someday, we might actually have something in common.* He called me to ask me to go on a double date with him and his wife with Scott as my date.

The night of the date I was scheduled to babysit for a family friend, but my sister agreed to watch the kids for me to be able to go on this first date with Scott. It was pretty cute how the boys—who were staying with my sister Misty at my parents' house—watched as Scott came to pick me up and commented on how he had a cool car and that he opened the door for me. My little men were looking out for me.

Our first date went very well. I remember that we both were able to talk pretty freely and effortlessly, but if you ask Scott, he says he couldn't

1

get a word in very often. I guess I was a little nervous.

Scott was busy finishing medical school and I was in my junior year of nursing school. By December, Scott found out he would officially graduate from medical school, and it was an exciting time. I had met him late in the process, but I knew it was still a great accomplishment for him as well as a struggle. God had blessed him with this, and it had become apparent this was part of God's will for Scott's life.

We dated exclusively for over a year when Scott had to move almost four hours away to start his residency. He hadn't matched with University of Virginia on the first time, but after some scrambling, the doors opened up for him to go there in the direction he thought God was leading. It was hard to see him move away, but we were confident neither of us was going anywhere, and that if God was in our relationship, He would work it all out so that we could be together again.

We emailed each other every day and were able to talk on the telephone once a week or so. Talk about tough times! Up until now, we had lived about ten minutes apart from each other and were able to talk on the telephone as much as we wanted for as long as we wanted. This was a big change in our relationship. Now, we were only able to see each other once every 4-6 weeks or so. If he came in to West Virginia, we would share the weekend with his family too.

While he was living in Charlottesville, Scott had visited many churches looking for the right one.

We had both been raised attending a Church of the Nazarene, so I encouraged him to give the one there a try. The first time he visited, he asked me to go along. I went, and the moment I walked in the front door, I felt a peace come over me as though I was at home. They were in between pastors at the time, so the attendance had dwindled down a little, and they had an interim preacher speaking. Come to find out, I knew of him. His in-laws attended my home church. Scott looked around and noticed the people were very friendly, but there weren't many young people his age there. He decided to keep looking and eventually tried a church that one of his coworkers attended. He was attending this larger church and loved it mostly because of his Sunday school class: singles.

I thought he should try the Nazarene church again since I had heard they now had a new pastor. He agreed to give it a try, so the next time I came down to visit, we attended the church together. Again, as I walked in the front door and was greeted by several ladies, I felt at home. I knew if I lived here, this was where I would attend. I just had to convince Scott.

After the service, we were able to meet the young pastor and his wife. He was gray-haired but very young. We went to lunch with them, and as I packed my car to head home, I asked Scott to try it again. In the next few weeks, he not only attended their services, but he had been to the one couple's house for dinner and played golf with the pastor and two other young men. The Lord had found Scott a church home as well as a few new friends. As I was able to come to visit, we both began to fall in love with the church and the great people there. We were forming a new church family.

As the months went on, Scott and I would talk more and more about getting married someday. In August 2000, Scott had taken a week off from work to come to West Virginia and visit everyone. I was so excited to be in the same town as him again if only for a week. One night after a church service Scott said that he wanted to talk. He had been thinking and had doubts about if I was the girl for him. His forever love. By the end of a very long conversation, he broke up with me saying that he needed some time to figure things out and that maybe time apart would help. I was devastated to say the least. By the time I drove myself home, I was hurt and mad. How dare he choose this week of all weeks to break up with me! Why didn't he do this next week after he went back to Charlottesville or even before he came in?! His last words were that he needed time, so right there, at a very early hour of the morning, I decided he could have all the time he wanted. If this was truly God's will for our lives, He would have to bring Scott back to me! I wouldn't call him or stop by to see him. He would get what he wanted all right! It was a tough week being all alone in my parents' home--they were still away at church camp--and having no one around to talk to. When I finally did get to tell my parents the news, I didn't want to cry in front of them, so I held it all in until later. I remember my dad telling me that if Scott was truly the man for me, God would bring him back. In the meantime, however, my daddy would be praying for me and for us. What a great daddy!

I spent the next three weeks praying for God's direction and resisting the urge to pick up the phone and call Scott. If he needed some time to answer his doubts about me, then that was fine. He would have to come back to me if he wanted to choose me. I wasn't going to make it easy on him and I certainly wasn't going to wait around forever. Finally, after three weeks of being broken up, Scott called me on the telephone and wanted to talk about us. It was so hard to listen and not be angry at him, but I did. He said he knew that he loved me and felt that he wanted to spend the rest of his life with me, but he was afraid. The behind-the-scenes story here is that he had been engaged to someone else years before and he was a little afraid to step out there again because this was going to be the only marriage for him. He asked me back, and from then on we have been together.

As a new college graduate, I had been working in the NICU as a registered nurse since June, and I was still in orientation still training to work in the NICU independently. It was a lot of pressure and I felt like I needed to be in one place for at least one year to learn my job and to be the best nurse I could be. Scott understood; he was just ready to be married and to live in the same town, much less the same house so that the long distance relationship could be over.

By the beginning months of 2001, Scott had begun talking about two different scenarios, "when we get married" and "if we get married." It was crazy. One conversation would include him wanting me to get an apartment in Charlottesville and work there and the next time it would be that he wasn't sure. At this point, we had already looked at engagement rings and he was still questioning whether I was the one God had intended for him to marry!

I went to Charlottesville to visit Scott on Saint Patrick's Day. I couldn't handle the back and forth of his words of hope and then doubt. It was Friday evening, March 16th, and Scott was at his house by the time I arrived. I knew he had something on his mind all throughout dinner that night because he was unusually quiet. I asked him several times if everything was okay, and he said yes. At that point, I figured he was tired from working all week and tried to let it go. By the time we finished dinner and went back to his house, he was back to his normal self and ready to watch a movie we had rented. At some point, Scott brought up the subject of marriage and how he thought I was the one God had kept for him as his life partner. I thought, *Here we go again*, and was ready to speak up and unload my thoughts on the subject to him when he pulled out a small present. I opened it and inside was a Disney princess flashing ring. I was clueless and thought this was a thoughtful gift, I guess. I was still figuring out what to say as a response to such a strange gift when he wanted to know if I would do him the honor of becoming his wife. Shocked and thinking he was joking, I responded with, "Well, it's going to take a better ring than that to secure my hand in marriage." So shallow, I know, but I was thinking he was teasing me on the marriage subject or that this was somehow going to become a promise ring. He then brought out a diamond ring and asked me if *this* ring would do the trick. Again, knowing Scott's personality as a jokester and our history, I quickly responded, "Well, that's not real." The look on his face said it all. I had crushed him with my disbelief of his proposal. He was serious and this was the moment I had dreamed about my whole life...I just didn't realize it! I said yes! Then, I had to call my parents.

By the next afternoon, we had time to sit down and talk about setting a date for our wedding. He said he didn't want a long engagement because he just wanted to start our life together now. He wanted to get married this summer because that would mark one year of experience for me as a registered nurse. We called the man I wanted to use as the photographer and learned he was available for July 21st. I knew then, that we would have our hands full, but that was going to be the day I would get to marry my best friend, Scott.

Chapter 2

MARRIED LIFE

We began planning for our wedding, calling to make many appointments from clothing to food and flowers. Both of us felt very strongly that along with planning for our special wedding day, we should also be preparing for our marriage. We began premarital counseling with my pastor via videotapes—yes, we were still using those back then! We would watch a video and follow along with the workbook on our own. After a few videotapes, we would meet in person with my pastor for a discussion and review. The series we used was by H. Norman Wright, *Before You Say "I Do."* Each of the lessons was insightful, but the one that really stuck with us both was the one concerning trusting God with your future together. He told his personal story of having to write his thesis on Down Syndrome children. Then, through a process of events, he later was chosen to lead a special class for children with Down Syndrome at his local church. Years later, he and his wife would have a child born with Down Syndrome. "You never know how God will use you in your life, but know that He is preparing you now for later," he said concluding his story. I didn't know why, but that lesson was the one that resonated in both of our minds. He also encouraged us to choose a life verse for our marriage. We could cling to it and these days as a reminder of where we began and God's promise for our life together. We chose Ephesians 2:22: "In Him you too are being built together to become a dwelling in which God lives by His Spirit."

We were married on July 21, 2001 in Charleston, West Virginia. It was an amazingly hot day that day, but I didn't care--I was marrying my best friend. We left on our honeymoon on Sunday morning. We were flying to San Juan and then boarding the Royal Caribbean cruise ship for a week-long cruise to the Southern Caribbean.

On our wedding night, as we drove to the hotel, Scott took out his wallet and placed it inside the car console. I told him he shouldn't do that because he might forget it, but he said he wouldn't because he did this all of the time. The next morning as we were getting in line at the airport to check into our flight, Scott realized he didn't have his wallet or photo ID! We checked in our suitcase, and while I went to the gate to wait, he called a taxi to get him back to the hotel where the car was parked. The plane started to board, and one after another, people were getting onto the airplane. I, however, was worried to death because there was no sign of Scott anywhere! I was just about to hand over our flight tickets when I saw Scott running towards our gate with all of his might. As we boarded the plane, they shut the door behind us. We were absolutely the last ones on the plane and the plane was ready to leave. I should have known then that this single event was an omen to our crazy life ahead.

We came home from our honeymoon and were excited to see our families again and to open our wedding presents with them. They wanted to see our pictures and hear about all of the fun excursions. After opening all of the presents, we knew it was time to load up our car and head to our new home together. This was the part I was dreading. I was moving nearly four hours from all of my family and friends for the first time. It was a teary goodbye to say the least and a quiet ride for most of the trip. I felt like a woman without a country.

Once in Charlottesville, Scott went back to work while I was at home all alone waiting for my nursing license to come into effect in the state of Virginia. The highlights of my days quickly became walking Scott's dog Lacy and getting the mail. When Scott would come home from work each evening, it was a race to see who could get to the door first, Lacy or me.

Finally I was able to go to work again. I had planned on going to work at the University of Virginia Hospital in the Neonatal Intensive Care Unit. As I continued to wait, I was growing more hesitant about working so many nights as a newlywed and someone who was new to town. My pastor's wife Lori was also a nurse and had applied for a job at a pediatrician's office. She mentioned she was interested in the part time job and that they were still looking for a full-time nurse. She gave me the contact information and I began praying about it. I didn't have much experience working with big kids, but I did love my pediatric rotations in nursing school. Scott and I talked about it and we both decided I could at least call and see what it would be like. I interviewed and they offered me a job. I was afraid to make this change, but I trusted God and felt this was the direction to go.

I started working in the pediatrician's office and fell in love with it! I was able to take care of children from birth through college here. My new friend Lori worked with me two days a week, and all of the other employees were friendly. I was finally placed with a female pediatrician to work, with and that made the job much more enjoyable. I was Dr. Alexander's nurse which meant I worked with her most days, and because of that, I was able to see many families and get to know them better. I would watch their children grow up before my eyes. That was perhaps the best part about my job. Feeling like I was making a difference in someone's life, even if for only a few minutes every now and then.

Our church was becoming like our home away from home. We were quickly getting involved with the young adults, and our church was growing. There were several couples we would hang out with. It seemed as though once a month we were having a baby shower or wedding shower to attend. We loved being a young married couple and learning more about each other. We were both busy with work, and I loved my job. I was learning more about how to care for children and having a great time.

By the winter of 2002, our lives were changing. Many of our friends were starting their families, and it was so much fun to have them over for dinner and to babysit their kids every now and then. Our best friends—who also happened to be our Pastor and wife, Bill and Lori—were trying to have another baby. Their only child was a little girl who was nine years old at the time. She was born with special needs and had consumed their time and energy with raising her. Up until now, they had been afraid to have another child. At some point, they both felt like it was time not to live in fear and to trust God for the outcome. They found out pretty quickly that they were pregnant only to lose that child in a miscarriage. They were devastated but still trusting God with their lives. I remember feeling so helpless. I wanted to take their hurt away, but I couldn't. A few months later, they tried again and found out they were indeed pregnant. Lori and I were able to go maternity clothes shopping, and I lived vicariously through her pregnancy.

The spring had passed and summer of 2003 was coming right along. Lori was starting to show, and by now everyone knew she was expecting. Our church family was thrilled and already thinking of the baby shower for our parsonage family. By that July, Lori noticed she was having contractions and went to the doctor. She was going into preterm labor at 18 weeks along. They sent her to the hospital to stay on bed rest indefinitely. I couldn't believe it! They couldn't lose this baby too! I went to visit Lori and "Shep"—as I had named our pastor because he was the shepherd of our flock—almost every day after work. Poor thing—she was forced to lie in a position called reverse Trendelenburg, where the head of her bed was lower than her feet. She stayed in the hospital and had ultrasounds every other day or so to evaluate the baby for about 3½ weeks. They discovered that her amniotic sac was bulging, which meant delivery was imminent. I did what I could to help my friends. I took Shep food as he needed it and ran a few errands for them so that he could stay at the hospital as much as possible. Many evenings, it was the three of us in Lori's hospital room trying to have a good time, while at the same time scared beyond belief at the possibility of the baby coming too soon. At that point, they knew if the baby had been born, that smaller hospital was not equipped to manage his life. They made the decision to change hospitals to one that had a level three NICU and could fully handle a micro-preemie if he was to be born so soon. It was now August 2003 and time was passing so slowly. On the morning of August 10, Jon Cooper Willis was born at almost 23 weeks gestation. He weighed one pound three ounces and was doing okay for now. The Lord had provided, but Cooper still had such a long road ahead.

My background was the NICU, so visiting him there wasn't a big deal to me. I wanted to check on him as much as possible and encourage our friends. While Lori was still in the hospital, we were alone in her room one evening and she asked me some tough questions. I don't know that I had the answers, but I do remember telling her that if it was me, I would want to celebrate every precious moment with my son while I still had him. So, that's just what they—we—did! Cooper had several surgeries while in the NICU, but eventually in December of 2003, he was discharged from the hospital and allowed to go home for the first time just days shy of his original due date! God is so good!

I thought long and hard about those days of uncertainty and felt at that time that I had fulfilled my purpose as best I could. God had placed me here with my background enabled me to answer a few questions and to encourage my friends at such a difficult and trying time in their lives. You never know how God will use you; you just have to be willing to be used.

Chapter 3

CHANGES

Somewhere between 2002 and 2003, we were beginning to think about where life would lead us after Scott's residency. We were falling in love with Charlottesville, Virginia. Our neighbors, our friends, our church family, everything there was fabulous. I felt like I had finally made Charlottesville my new home and was very happy there. Outside of our church friends, we also had a wonderful street where we lived that was filled with wonderful friends and neighbors. To move away from this to another unknown place seemed crazy to me. At the same time, Scott knew that there were no positions available for him when he would finish residency. The reality that we might not be able to stay there became more real every day.

Scott didn't want a research position and wanted to spend more time with patients but at the same time still be able to have a family life at home outside of work. This narrowed the search some because he knew he didn't want an academic job. He went to his yearly meetings looking for jobs. He came back with a few prospects and was the most interested in one at home in Charleston, West Virginia and one in Kingsport, Tennessee. Well, the choice was very easy for me—we were going home! If we couldn't stay in Charlottesville in our new home, then we should go back to what we knew. At least there we had friends, family, and my former job in the NICU. The only negative I could even come up with was that we would have to decide on a church to attend. When we had lived there, we both attended different churches because we weren't married. He had his church and I had mine—my home church that I had attended for sixteen years before getting married. If that was the biggest obstacle to moving home, then I was confident we could overcome that and make a decision.

Scott wasn't so sure and felt like we needed to take a look around at both areas. Charleston was easy; we knew the area well enough that we didn't need to meet a realtor or anyone else to show us around. We planned a trip home to visit our families, and while we were there, Scott met with the physicians at that hospital to talk about a perspective job. We simply drove around in the evenings in the neighborhoods looking at homes and praying as we went. We were somewhat used to the higher cost of living in Charlottesville, so the house prices and taxes didn't scare us. We knew the areas we liked. We didn't go into any of the homes, but looking at the neighborhoods and the exteriors of the houses was good enough. Of course I wanted God's will for our lives, but I still wanted most desperately to move home.

We were also going to make a trip to Kingsport, Tennessee. He had only been home a few weeks from the convention, but it was all he could think or talk about. I would find Scott researching the area on the internet a lot. It really drove me nuts to see him so excited about possibly moving again to some new place and starting over. I couldn't figure out what was so appealing about Kingsport. It wasn't that it was a bad place in my opinion; I just didn't understand why it looked so much better than moving home? We knew Charleston; it was my home and very close to his home as well.

Off to Kingsport we went. We could only stay two days there to look around and Scott would be on an all-day interview for one of them. While he was there, I was scheduled to ride around with someone to look at houses and get to know the area a little better. I did, and we saw a lot. Again, I didn't go into any of the houses, but I did see many areas that reminded me of my hometown and in particular the street where my parents lived. I found myself liking the area enough because it reminded me a lot of Charleston. Kingsport was definitely a little smaller of a town and more laid back, but that could be a good thing. We had dinner that evening with the doctors and their wives as well as a few other physicians and their spouses from the hospital. We had a great time and were happy to meet new people. The pressure, of course, was on for me because I knew Scott really liked the two men he would work with if we took this position. I had to find a few things to like about the area too. It was a wonderful evening, even if it wasn't my hometown.

The next morning, Scott wanted to look around town at some of the houses and neighborhoods I had seen. His potential boss had given us a name and phone number of the realtor they had used to purchase their home. This lady was so sweet to take us around for half of the day without forcing us to sign any papers to lock her in as our realtor. We learned she was a Christian, and it made it actually a fun day getting to know Kim while looking at houses. We already knew that we liked looking at homes and getting decorating ideas, but this was different. When you are newly married and have limited funds to go out on dates, you come up with some crazy ideas! One of which for us became looking at houses and model homes in our area. God had given us this day to have fun and just be a couple looking at the potential for our future, but I knew—or so I thought—down deep this could be a big waste of time. However, I could definitely sense that Scott was ready to sign the papers on moving here if he was offered a job.

The following summer, the office in Kingsport offered Scott the opportunity to work as a locum (a person who temporarily fulfills the duties of another) for one week in their office as kind of a way to have a week-long interview. He spent the days learning how they performed their jobs and the evenings going around town with Kim, the same realtor we used this past fall, looking at houses. "At least give it a try, Kristi," he would say. "I think it is a great opportunity."

The more Scott talked about Tennessee, the

more upset I was becoming with him and with the whole situation. God could work this issue out and let us stay in Charlottesville or better yet, I thought, move us back to our families. Each time I would present the positives of moving back home and accepting a job there, it seemed like Scott could find three more positives towards the job in Tennessee. How could he possibly ask me to do this? I had already moved away from everything I knew into a strange new place for him once, and now he wanted me to do it again! I couldn't believe he was asking me to consider this move! At the same time, I was praying that God would open the doors for us that needed to be opened and close the ones that needed closing. Why wasn't he closing Kingsport? God couldn't possibly want us to move again and start all over. Scott and I would get to the point of where we had to agree to disagree and change the subject. When you and your spouse are both a little stubborn, you quickly come to realize that no one is going to "win" the topic and sometimes; it's best to leave it alone for a while and readdress it a little later when we could calm down and pray about it.

We had been asking our friends to pray for us concerning this decision as well as our marriage. That we could not only discern God's will for us, but also that both of us would have a peace about where we were headed. That we could trust God completely with everything in our new transitions, wherever they may be. We could sense their prayers and trusted that God, in His time, would show us the direction to move.

One day, I was griping to my friend Lori

about all of this and was very worried that Scott was talking about Tennessee a whole lot more than he was talking about West Virginia. She calmly let me rant to her, and then she said to me, "What if God is testing you in this area, Kristi? What if moving you out of your comfort zone is what it will take for you to completely trust not only God, but also that Scott, as your husband, is capable of seeking God's will for your lives together?" That hit me like a ton of bricks! I really didn't want to hear that, but for whatever reason, it stuck with me, and I had to pray differently from then on. I had been praying that God would let Scott see that we needed to move back to where I was comfortable, my home, my former job in the NICU, my ways, instead of where God would guide Scott. Talk about a tough prayer to pray! You know you have to do something that every part of your human self tells you that you don't want to do, but at the same time you know in order to obey God you have to surrender to what He wants. I knew that God's ways are always better than our ways, but knowing it and actually acting on it are two entirely different things. Why would He want us to start over again with jobs, houses, friends, and a church home? I didn't understand any of it. I was too close to the situation. I was praying with my interests at heart. I said that I was concerned with God's will, but when I started to think and mull over what Lori had told me, I began to realize I might have been praying with the wrong attitude. With all of these questions running around freely in my mind, I still had an underlying peace that no matter where we landed, God would put us exactly where he wanted us. I knew He would make a way where there seemed to me to be no way.

In the fall of 2003, Scott officially signed a contract to accept the job in Kingsport, TN. I was still unsure about this move and starting over completely, but I trusted my husband and my God that this was what was best for us. We celebrated, just the two of us, in our little home in Charlottesville. I had cooked a special meal for us and used our wedding china! I took pictures of Scott signing the contract to mark it as a new beginning for Scott and Kristi.

Who knew that later that month, we would discover that our other project we had been working on would be on its way? We found out in late October that we were pregnant with our first child. What an exciting and scary time for our family of soon-to-be three! I am very old fashioned, I guess, but I didn't want to tell anyone about our pregnancy until we had our first ultrasound and saw our baby's heartbeat. During all of this time, it was so exciting knowing we had a little secret that for a little while longer, no one else knew but us!

Somewhere during all of this, we would have a house to sell in Charlottesville, a house to purchase in Kingsport, and to prepare for a really big move. Where would we find the time? I wasn't sure, but I knew that God's timing was perfect and that He would provide the time. One evening, we were meeting our friends, Shep and Lori for a quick dinner before going to the NICU to visit their son. We met up for dinner and out of the blue, Shep looked at me and asked, "Kristi, are you pregnant yet?" I guess the look on my face gave it all away. Lori had known because I had to tell someone at work. She hadn't told him yet, and besides her, Scott was the only other person who knew. Scott simply smiled, and then we asked them not to tell anyone else. We hadn't even told our families yet, but had already begun to plan a way to surprise them with the news! It's really neat how God provided us with a set of lifelong friends whom we could share such life changing experiences with and know what a treasure we were to each other.

Sometime in November, we traveled back to Kingsport to get serious about house hunting. We met up with Kim, our realtor, again and were able to look at several homes. We were looking a little differently this time. We had to look for places with enough room for our new little one and visiting family members since we would live so far away from them all.

We were only able to spend a few days there looking around, so once we came back to Charlottesville, we sold our house. The same day our house in Charlottesville sold, Scott was ready to put an offer in on the house I really wanted. The more we had prayed about it, the neater things fell together. We knew we needed a place to grow our family and a place that could be our forever home. God had led us to this place; getting this house was going to be a small detail for Him to work out. God had touched my heart and given me a deep settled peace about this move, and I was actually a little excited about it! Of course, the human part of me was a nervous wreck, but I was confident to trust in

God's plan.

By Thanksgiving, we had our first ultrasound and were able to see our baby's heartbeat! It was such an exciting time in our lives! We made copies of the ultrasound pictures and had plans of how to surprise our families with the exciting news at Thanksgiving. God was truly blessing us by moving us in the center of His will.

Thanksgiving came and went and our families were so excited for us. Another grandbaby was on the way for Scott's family and the first grandbaby was coming to my parents. My pregnancy was going well and I was feeling great. Christmas was coming and we were planning our move to Kingsport. Everything seemed to be happening at once. A house to settle, new jobs for both of us, and a new baby on the way!

We decided not to get a Christmas tree since we were moving a few days after New Year's. It was pretty sad for me, I have to admit. I knew it made more sense to skip the Christmas decorations for one year so that it would be less on our list to pack up, but it just didn't feel like Christmas. Our friends surprised us by bringing over a "baby tree." It was a tabletop tree decorated with pink and blue flowers and baby stuff. There were miniature strollers, bottles and bibs as decorations. It made my Christmas special that year.

We were able to travel back to West Virginia to spend some time at Christmas with both of our families. It was a nice retreat from the craziness that was going on in our lives. Once back in Virginia to pack up and finish working, I also had to go to the doctor one more time before moving. It was a good visit and showed that so far, our baby was growing very well and the pregnancy was moving along right like it should be. We were able to be in our house for New Year's Eve all alone to spend the rest of 2003 as Virginians and start the beginning of 2004 before we had to move to Kingsport. It was a nice few days to reminisce our newlywed years there and see our friends one last time. I wanted to be here as long as I could. The peace I had previously felt was somehow diminishing. I was afraid that the people in Tennessee wouldn't love us the way our church family here did. I had to let my fears go a little and keep reminding myself of God's promises. That He would take care of us and that He was moving us to where He wanted us to be. Everything would somehow work out. If I had learned anything in life thus far, I knew that God's timing is perfect. He can be trusted.

Chapter 4

NEW LIFE IN TENNESSEE

Our first few days in Tennessee were pretty busy. I was hard at work trying to unpack our house while Scott was busy working on getting our gas turned on downstairs. It was the beginning of January, and it was cold. We would wear our coats to unpack what we could all day and then spend the evening and night upstairs in our bedroom where we did have heat. Looking back on it now, it is a little funny that we had those snags and had to adapt so quickly. After a few days, everything was turned on and working properly.

I was still waiting for my Tennessee nursing license to arrive, but still going through the motions of pursuing a job in the NICU. I was interested in working per diem or at least being on the registry. I knew this would keep me busy as well as keep my nursing skills up. The extra money would be nice as well. An interview and hospital tour was scheduled for me and I was pretty excited. I went through with the blood work and physical. A few days later they called me back to say my blood work showed I wasn't immune to measles, mumps, and rubella (MMR). It wasn't a big deal. It would just require another MMR vaccination before I could safely work in the hospital environment. The only problem was that the MMR vaccination is a live virus, and I couldn't safely take it now that I was pregnant. It just felt like the right thing to do was for me to stay at home for the rest of my pregnancy. I felt very guilty about not helping out financially to our family, but somehow, there was a peace about it and everything else would work out.

By the end of January, we were settling into a new routine of life here in Kingsport. It was Sunday morning and we were up getting ready for church. After my shower and while fixing my hair, I started to feel nauseated and hot as if I would pass out. I tried to tell myself it was probably something I had eaten the night before, but it didn't seem to get any better. I spent most of the day in the bed with side pain and weak feeling. It was hard for me to walk freely without pain or sit up for very long. I was scared to death that I was going to miscarry this precious baby. I just remember Scott and me praying that this baby was a gift from the Lord, and if He wanted to take this baby, He could. We desperately wanted to have this little boy or girl to raise, but we submitted fully to His plan and that day confirmed that the baby was in His hands. I had a doctor's appointment in two days, so as long as I was doing okay, we were going to stick it out at home. By my appointment, we discovered two things: the doctor that we were meeting for the appointment had actually went to medical school with Scott and I had a mass inside my right ovary that was called a teratoma. As long as my pain was under control, the plan was to wait for surgery to remove it after the baby was born. In the event that I would need a cesarean section, they could remove it then. I knew I would have to go home and research this one, but the thought of needing surgery while I was still pregnant scared me to death! Once again, I knew my God was in complete control. There was a gentle underlying peace that if He could give us a familiar face for a doctor, then He could take care of this pain and control the teratoma until it was safe to remove it. Our baby was still growing very well and looked like he or she should at this point. The icing on the cake for me that day was getting to hear my baby's heartbeat one more time. I needed this assurance and the Lord provided. It would be two more weeks until our next ultrasound, and it was then that we learned we were being blessed with a daughter! As soon as I left the appointment, I went straight to the mall and purchased my baby girl's first dress. I had so much fun!

It seemed like the time flew by that spring. Scott was busy studying for his board exams and I was getting ready for a little girl to arrive. That day finally came on Monday, July 5, 2004, at 5:37pm. Kerri Elizabeth Coen was born; to us she was the most beautiful baby in the world. It was a great feeling to hold this most precious gift from God created just for us. It was a special time for us to learn who this sweet little baby was, what she liked and what seemed to calm her. It was a wonderful time for Scott and me both to see our parenting styles in full force. Of course, we had several issues arise from our differences and other influences, but through it all, God was faithful to us and ever-so-close to help us through this time of transition into new roles.

Chapter 5

THREE BECOMES FOUR

Scott and I had always talked about wanting a lot of children if the Lord so blessed. He always said he wanted four children, and I knew I wanted more than two. Along with this, we also knew we wanted our children to be close in age. My sister and I were 23 months apart, and I thought that was great. So a few months after Kerri's first birthday, we were ready for our family of three to grow to become a family of four. In November 2005 we were so thrilled to learn that we were in pregnant with baby number two. This baby was our little secret for now, and we were already thinking of a creative way to tell our families. With a background as a NICU nurse, I just knew too many things that could go wrong early in pregnancy, so I wanted to wait until we saw and heard the heartbeat before we told anyone. By Christmas time, we were ready to tell our awesome secret We made photo calendars for both sets of our parents as a present to open. In the month of August, we placed an ultrasound picture of this baby because this was the month the baby was due. All of the other months were filled with pictures of Kerri. The funny thing was that neither one of our mothers caught onto it when they first opened the calendar. They both thought that the ultrasound picture was of Kerri! We had to offer a few hints to both of them to clue them in that they were in fact becoming grandparents again. This baby was already a blessing and would definitely bring more happiness and joy to everyone we loved.

My pregnancy was progressing very well and similar to Kerri's. I had moved on into my second trimester and was feeling less tired and ready to know more about this precious baby growing in my belly. We both felt like this baby was going to be another little girl, but we couldn't be sure until our ultrasound. I remember counting down the days until we had our "anatomy ultrasound" at the 20 week mark of pregnancy for baby number two on March 8, 2006. The night before I hadn't slept very well and had several bad dreams that something was wrong with this baby. I couldn't be sure, but I just knew something was going to be wrong. I am a worrier by nature, so it could've been just that, but for whatever reason, I was excited for this day while dreading it at the same time.

We went to the doctor for the ultrasound. My fears were founded when the technician scanned over the baby's legs. I knew they didn't look right, but wasn't sure if it was club feet or something different. That is one of the bad things about being a nurse or in the medical field; you know a little bit about most things, but seemingly not enough to know for certain when it is your own. The ultrasound tech went to get my doctor to have him take a look at the ultrasound, and I remember telling Scott to keep recording the ultrasound because I wanted to celebrate this baby's life while we had it, but also because we would need to catch everything they were going to tell us in the next few minutes. When my doctor came back into the room, it was strange; here was a friend of ours now having to tell us some potentially bad news. I felt so bad for him, but I was so anxious and needed to know what we were dealing with. While the technician and my doctor were scanning my belly, I was thinking like they were. I was thinking I need to see the head and neck area and they would scan that area. It was like I was taking an active part in processing my child from head to toe without saying a word. We were working in sync. By the end of a very long ultrasound session, we didn't have many answers, but we did know we were in fact having another little girl. They thought the baby might have club feet of some type, but also that she had something wrong with her legs as well. They made an appointment for us to see the high-risk obstetrician the next week and warned us that they would be asking us if we wanted to terminate the pregnancy. I was shocked. I already knew our answer was no, but couldn't get past the fact that they would ask anyway. In that moment, our faith would be tested. We always said we would trust God with whatever came our way, and now it looked like something very different was about to happen with our second child. I couldn't get out of the office fast enough that day. I was trying to process everything that had been told to us while at the same time trying to be strong enough not to lose it in the hospital lobby. We took our time going home because my mom was there with Kerri, and we knew she along with the rest of our families were anxious to hear what we were having.

Once home, we were able to make the appropriate phone calls to our families and tried to move on as much as possible. We wouldn't know anything for another week, so what could all of the worrying do? By bedtime, Scott and I wanted to research a few possibilities, so we did what every healthcare professional would tell you not to do: we looked on the internet for answers. We didn't really find anything to latch on to, so we decided to turn off the computer and spend some time alone together. We prayed and asked God to watch over this special baby that was growing inside of me and reminded ourselves that this baby was His child. We were only the parents chosen to hopefully raise this most precious gift. Her little life was in His hands, and He could do with her whatever He so chose. This brought us such peace that night. I cannot fully describe it, but in the midst of such heartache, there was peace.

We pulled out the baby name books that night and came across Sydnee. This name means "dedicated." We also liked Danielle, which means "God is my judge." We liked this name when we were expecting Kerri, but it just didn't seem to fit. There were other names we liked, but Sydnee Danielle just seemed right. With this name she would have my middle name and her daddy's initials, SDC. In case she wouldn't survive, she now had a name, and if we couldn't have any more children, both girls had a form of my name, which was something Scott felt strongly about. We wouldn't tell anyone her name until she was born, but for now, we were going to celebrate every day we had with her. We were definitely scared to death, but we were fully trusting God for His will in her life.

On Sunday, we went to our church with heavy hearts. We knew our friends there would have many questions that we just didn't have the answers to. We had already told everyone everything we knew but tried to remain strong and answer their questions to the best of our abilities. We told our pastor we wanted to be anointed as a full trust in God for His complete healing of our baby's body if that was His will. Again, there was such peace and comfort being surrounded by our church family and all of them praying for our family. What a blessing to behold! It was in the sermon on that morning that I was led to Psalm 139:13-16.

> *You created my inmost being; you knit me together in my mother's womb. I praise You because I am fearfully and wonderfully made; Your works are wonderful, I know that full well. My frame was not hidden from You when I was made in the secret place, when I was woven together in the depths of the earth. Your eyes saw my unformed body;*

all the days ordained for me were written in your book before one of them came to be.

These special verses would become Sydnee's life verses. This was our prayer for her young life, that all of her days were ordained before one of them came to be. It was a comfort knowing that long before this day God knew about what was going to happen and He had everything under control. We could rest in that peace and assurance knowing He hadn't forgotten about us.

At the high-risk obstetrician's appointment we were scheduled for an amniocentesis (the sampling of amniotic fluid from the uterus to screen for developmental abnormalities in a fetus). I was very nervous about the procedure but knew we needed to do it to get more answers. They asked a lot of questions about our family histories especially our pregnancies. It was a very emotionally draining process and difficult to think about both of our families and any issues that might have gone wrong with any of those pregnancies. They did, in fact, ask us if we were considering terminating this pregnancy. I was ready for them to ask and was able to answer with absolute certainty, "No." If this was the child that God had given us, then we would love it to the best of our ability. It wasn't our decision to end a life. That alone belonged to God. It was a long day to say the least. The doctor said she felt the baby could have a rare syndrome called Klippel-Trenaunay-Weber syndrome. She explained that the results of the amnio would tell us more, but for now, if this was what it was, it was in the lymphedema family. She said the right leg was slightly larger and longer than the left one. There was a sixth toe on her left foot, and we wouldn't be sure until the results came back and we had more testing. For now, I became more determined than ever to fight for this precious girl. We left there knowing that our lives were changing more than we thought. We would have many, many appointments during this pregnancy to many specialists, and we would have to get organized and stay on top of all of the information.

The next four weeks passed by in such a blur. We had been to four appointments to various doctors trying to find out as much information as possible about our baby girl on the way. By 23 weeks, we were heading to Vanderbilt University for a new doctor to take a look at me and the baby via ultrasound as well as to meet with the genetics team there to figure this out. It was a big trip for us, and we were so hopeful for any information that we could find. This had been a whirlwind of a month for us, and I was ready for some definite answers. I was still in a place emotionally where my world was turned upside down, but I was trusting in God to carry us through this. I had been taught to always depend on God for any circumstance that I may find myself in. He knew all about this sweet baby girl because He created her just for us. After all, in God's eyes, this baby is absolutely perfect! With His help, we were determined to raise her in the fear and reverence of the Lord for whatever time we had with her in utero or out.

While trying to stay positive, I also found

myself wishing for the perfect pregnancy. I would be in the doctor's office waiting for my routine monthly appointments and listening to the other women complain about their backs hurting and saying how they wished their pregnancies were over. I remember thinking, *Wow, if you only knew how lucky you are!* It bothered me so, sitting there listening to them complain. I remember at times feeling like I had a dark storm cloud over my head, and it moved with me wherever I went. I knew our friends at church all meant well, but it seemed like our appointments were every Wednesday, and that meant we were expected to have more information to share with them that evening in church. It was at times too much and too many questions to answer. My only coping mechanism was to skip church that night with Scott at home spending family time together laughing at Kerri's funny faces or just being silly. That was the best medicine for me those days. At each of these doctor appointments, I would have an ultrasound where it just happened that they would spend the majority of the time focusing on the "bad" parts of this baby and not enough time letting me hear her precious heartbeat or see her sweet profile on the screen. I remember leaving these appointments feeling so low and full of fear and concern for the future. At one point, I guess my obstetrician sensed I was growing tired of all of these appointments, and he offered to cancel his regular appointments. He said he could use the measurements and ultrasounds from the high risk OB's office. I was adamant that I needed the appointments with his office because if there wasn't anything wrong with this baby, those would be the only appointments I would have. I needed to feel "normal." This was my normal if that even existed anymore.

By the third trimester of my pregnancy, it was still a crazy time of guessing how things would go and where we could deliver the baby. All of the details were still up in the air and no one really had solid answers for us to go on. I went back to the high risk OB at about 28 weeks and was scheduled to meet a visiting doctor who was there on a locum for my doctor. She was amazed that we didn't have a game plan. She was obviously a go-getter because she felt we should get the ball rolling. She knew what I had felt all along: this baby could come at any time and we weren't ready. No one would know what to do when this baby comes, including us! She suggested sending our records to a doctor at Boston Chidren's Hospital. She said she was from Connecticut and had another patient a few years ago with Klippel-Trenaunay-Weber syndrome. What an answer to many prayers for us! We had been praying all along for God's will in this situation but didn't know what to do next. She gave us the name of a physician in Boston who was familiar with this, and we left there with more hope than we had felt in quite a while. How amazing that we had never met her before today and that she would have some knowledge about the baby's syndrome and would know how to help us! It was just another assurance that God's timing was absolutely perfect.

That evening we jumped onto the internet to look up this Boston physician and were surprised to see exactly who he was. Scott had been to a conference about a year ago and a speaker talked about a man who was doing a lot of research in tumor development concerning the blood supply. The person had spoken a lot about this man's research and how they were implementing it into vascular anomalies research. Come to find out, Scott had wondered about this doctor from Boston before today and had again come across his name in this research. At the same time the visiting physician was here in Tennessee, the Vanderbilt physicians were thinking of sending us to Boston, and Scott had come across the research to wonder if we needed to go to Boston to get more answers.

Journal entry: May 19, 2006

Sweet girl, tonight was a hard evening for me. Daddy has been busy studying a lot lately and Kerri Beth and I have had to do a lot on our own. We went shopping today and ran a few errands. While at the mall, there were so many small babies and mothers to look at. All of the baby clothes were so cute. I thought about you all day on and off. I saw so many cute clothes and shoes for infants. I am afraid to buy anything because I don't know if you will be able to wear any of them. They say one of your legs is longer than the other one and that your feet are wider and perhaps have extra toes which makes regular shoes to fit hard to find. I worry about if you are in pain or if you don't know any different. Will people look at you and make fun of you as you get older? I also worry if I will be upset by the appearance of your leg and side. I feel very guilty for having these concerns, but they are true feelings. I pray that God will help me to deal with all of this. I love you, sweet girl, with all of my heart. I know that God created you in His image and that you are perfect in His eyes. In my heart, I am okay with everything. Whatever God wills is fine, but in my head, I worry about everyone else and their reactions. What a silly thing to worry about! This hard day progressed through the evening when I looked on the internet for pictures. Of course, they have very difficult pictures to look at and may not truthfully represent what we are dealing with ourselves. I found myself crying over these pictures because of heartbreak and worry over you and what you may have to face in your precious life. Rest assured, sweet one, your life is in God's hands and we accept whatever He wills. With His help, we will be strong because He has promised to help us every step of the way. May you continue to grow strong and in God's hands. I love you with all of my heart. I am anxiously awaiting your arrival to meet this precious gift God has placed inside of me. Until then, I will do the best I can to find the best care for you. You are our blessing, sweet one! Love, Mommy

The day was finally here that the Boston physician Dr. Fishman was planning to call us and talk with us via conference call about our baby girl. He was the one with the most experience treating Klippel-Trenaunay-Weber patients along the East Coast, so we knew if anyone knew anything about the syndrome, he would be the best one to get answers from. I was 30 weeks pregnant now and getting more anxious to find out answers or get a better game plan formed. He was so patient to talk with us and let us ask as many questions as possible. Based on our ultrasounds, fetal MRI, and other records, he also agreed that our baby definitely had Klippel-Trenaunay-Weber syndrome. He said that she definitely had large feet and at least one extra toe on the left foot and perhaps more on the right. He said that neurologically everything was fine and that this would involve her physically only. Our biggest question was if he thought the baby was or would be in any pain because of the syndrome. He said that in his experience, most of the patients didn't complain about pain as much as heaviness in the affected area. What a relief and answered prayer for us! In our research, we had come across information that said pain was associated with this rare syndrome. The thought of our daughter being in pain a lot worried us greatly. He continued to tell us that when the baby was born, she could be delivered naturally and should be without complications. He told us that she shouldn't need any extra tests performed once she is here, and that she could stay in the newborn nursery like any other newborn baby. All along, we wondered if we would need to deliver our baby in a bigger medical center or children's hospital due to her syndrome. He said no, but our main focus after she was born was taking her home and getting to know her. What a relief! Things were looking up for us, even if they were just small things. He concluded that he would like us to come to Boston with our baby once she was about three months old, and he could get a better look at her and go from there. With this information on board, we now had to finish getting prepared for our little one to arrive. He said his office would send us a few pictures of patients with Klippel-Trenaunay-Weber that was similar to what he thought our daughter would have in order for us to get a better idea of what to expect. "Until then," he said, "just enjoy the pregnancy."

By 35 weeks, I went to my routine appointment with my obstetrician. It was the appointment where they do the test to check for Group B strep. Because of this, he went ahead and checked me and said I was only a fingertip dilated. Not to worry, though, I should be okay for another few weeks or so. This was good news because we were planning to travel to West Virginia this weekend to celebrate Kerri's 2nd birthday a few days early with both of our families. On Saturday, July 1, 2006, we had a wonderful 2nd birthday party for our first princess, Kerri Beth. It was extremely hot outside and by the evening, I was feeling worn out! I went to bed exhausted, but woke up around 3:30 in the morning in a panic. I thought I had either lost control of my bladder or my water had broken! I ran to the restroom only to realize the liquid was dark which meant only one thing, blood. This wasn't good, and I needed help. I woke Scott up and we were quickly on our way to the emergency room there in West Virginia! I was scared to death, but also, strangely calm. I guess this was where I was beginning to realize I wasn't in control. After being admitted, they scooted me off to the basement of the hospital for an ultrasound to check on the baby. At this point, the doctors were worried that I was abrupting, which could be a bad thing. The pain was starting to come as well as the fears. I wasn't sure if I was going to have an emergency cesarean section or if I would stay here a few days and end up on bed rest. I did know, however, that going into labor at 35 weeks pregnant wasn't a good thing. Along with her syndrome, we could now also be facing prematurity issues.

In times of great stress, I tend to find comfort in the small things. It just happened that, yes, we were out of town and going to the hospital where no one knew anything about our precious girl, but it was the hospital where I had worked as a nurse in the NICU, and my sister worked in labor and delivery and mother/baby as a nurse. It was my home town, and I knew whatever happened, the Lord was definitely watching out for us. In case we needed to go to the NICU, I still knew several of the workers there as well as the physicians.

I had dialated to three centimeters, so I was indeed in labor. The rest of the morning was spent talking to many doctors there including the neonatalogist to let them know a little about what we had been told about the baby's syndrome. I was placed on bed rest to make sure the bleeding would stop. By this time, the news had spread and we had visitors starting to show up at the hospital. It had been a crazy morning, but it now looked like this was going to be the day our precious baby girl would be born.

After a long day of visitors and lying in the bed, our precious baby girl made her way into the world at 8:35 pm. She looked beautiful as her daddy helped deliver her and became the first human hands to hold her. At this sweet moment, those present in the room were so happy. I wanted to see this sweet girl with my own eyes. I remember Dr. Lowery and the nurse saying, "Kristi, it's not that bad." From what I could tell, she looked just like they had told us she might. Her face and arms were so tiny. Her right leg was larger and longer than the left and she had a purple port wine stain covering the lateral aspect of the leg. Her left leg was more proportionate with a wide foot and an extra toe almost like a skin tag. I wanted so desperately to hold her and love on her, but I knew she needed to be evaluated by the NICU team. They took a quick look and listen to her and said she looked good. Dr. Lowery, the neonatologist on call, winked at me and said they were going to take her to the NICU to observe. I think he was protecting us a little and by taking her over there; she wouldn't have as many people looking at her as most babies are in the cribs in front of the window for all to see. I had to wait until about 10:30 that night to get to go to the NICU and see her at her bedside. It was so painful to be without her, but I knew without a doubt that she was in good hands. By this time, we had announced to our families that her name was Sydnee Danielle

Coen. They loved it! We told them the meaning of her name and that she had a part of my name and her daddy's initials. It was a special time to celebrate the miracle that she was.

I wasn't able to hold my precious girl until the next day. My arms were aching to hold her and snuggle with her. It was such a precious moment when the nurse placed her into my arms. Sydnee spent six days in the NICU because she was acting like a typical preemie. She became jaundiced and had to go under phototherapy lights. Also, they didn't let her eat until they had scanned everything out. They were new to her and hadn't been given much information on what to expect prior to her birth. The testing revealed that she had hydronephrosis (swelling due to a backup of urine) in her left kidney. While there, they also discovered she had a heart murmur and then an ASD, an atrial septal defect (a rare disorder of the heart that is present at birth and involves a hole in the wall that separates the two upper chambers of the heart). We were so thankful she stayed here those six days so that we could learn this about her. On top of Boston doctors for the syndrome, we would also be juggling a pediatric cardiologist and a nephrologist. They were also able to remove the extra toe from her left foot while we were there before being discharged. It was a crazy week to juggle being a mommy to Kerri who had her actual birthday this week while her new sister was in the NICU, trying to visit the NICU to be with Sydnee as much as possible, and managing all of this while my husband went back to work. It was a tough week on all of us.

Saturday morning, Sydnee's nurse called me and said she had heard a murmur while she was listening to Sydnee's heart sounds. They wanted to do a cardiac workup on her to make sure everything was okay. When we arrived at the hospital, we were able to talk with the pediatric cardiologist, and she confirmed that Sydnee did in fact have an ASD and that it looked okay right now, but we would need to follow up with a cardiologist in our area. We were finally able to bring our daughter to my parents' house that afternoon. She was six days old now and had a big sister there who desperately wanted to see her. We sent word that we were on our way, and Kerri was on the front porch waiting to see "Baby Syd" as she called her. Kerri was the first person there to hold Sydnee that day, and what a sweet moment it was! Kerri would smile and pat Sydnee's belly. It was absolutely precious to watch. Both of our grandmothers were there and were able to hold and officially meet Sydnee Danielle. It was wonderful to have our families and friends there to celebrate such a special day. It had been a long week, one that was started and finished with great celebrations.

Chapter 6

TWO CHILDREN UNDER TWO

On Sunday, we loaded up our car as well as my mom's van and headed off to Tennessee. Nana, my mom, was able to come along with us for a few days to help out. Sydnee's room was ready, but I still had a cradle to bring out, a few baby clothes to wash and a car full of birthday presents to unload. It took us a little longer than usual to get home that day. We quickly learned that traveling with a newborn and a two-year-old takes a while. We made it home safely to find a beautifully decorated yard welcoming our precious little one! With Kerri, I had ordered balloons and decorations ahead of time for my family to place in our house when she was born. With the chaos of Sydnee's early birth, I was heartbroken that I wouldn't have the same welcome home for Sydnee. Thanks again to a wonderful set of family and friends, our yard was decorated with a beautiful shade of pink!

Life continued to be very busy for us in the next few weeks learning to juggle doctors' appointments as well as dealing with a second child. My mom was able to stay with us for a few weeks to help out and to get us to and from doctor appointments. Sydnee had a precipitous delivery, which just meant she came out pretty fast. Because of this, her little face was bruised for about two weeks. Poor thing, she looked like she had been in a fight and lost. Finally, all of the bruising went away as well as the jaundice. By this time, we were getting into a routine of normal activities. Life was crazy busy, but it was super fun. One evening, we had just finished giving both girls a bath and dried their hair. We were heading out of our bedroom and on our way to take the girls to their bedrooms for bed. I was carrying Sydnee in my arms and evidently Kerri was walking right underneath my arms. Sydnee started to spit up, so I leaned her over so that it could go onto the hardwood floor and not our clothes. Well, it went all over our clothes as well as Kerri's hair! Scott and I couldn't do anything but laugh because we knew we had to repeat everything we had just finished. Kerri Beth, on the other hand, just stood there and cried. It was special memories like this that kept us going. It was a busier life now with two little girls, but we were so full of joy!

By the middle of August of 2006, Sydnee was six weeks old, and we traveled to our church camp in West Virginia. At the end of the week, they had a healing service. It is our belief that God could fully heal my Sydnee if He so chose. In this service, Scott and I both felt led to have Sydnee anointed for God's will in her life whatever that may be. Of course, the desires of our hearts were for her complete healing and that she wouldn't have to be different or deal with all that she was going to face. But we had to remind ourselves that she is God's child and just on loan to us. She was in His hands and we wanted His complete will for her young life. It was more about wanting His will than our way.

We spent the first few months monitoring Sydnee's weight gain, going to her cardiologist, and visiting the pediatric nephrologist. We were keeping tabs on the hydronephrosis in her left kidney as well as the ASD in her heart. Because of her preemie size and the fact that she was jaundiced when she was born, the nephrologist wanted to start her on preventative antibiotics for four months to get her through the winter months. I was so upset that she was going to have to start them so early, but it would help keep her heathy.

Sydnee was nearing two and a half months old now, and we had planned her dedication ceremony. The ceremony symbolized us rededicate-ing our daughter to God publically. That she was His child and was in His hands. We certainly wouldn't be able to handle the challenges each day without His help.

Excerpt from Journal dated Sunday, Oct 8, 2006:

You are our special blessing from God, Sydnee. We know that you have always been in God's hands, and today we rededicated you to Him publically. God is going to use your sweet life in a wonderful way. I know you are going to be a special testimony of His love and grace. We love you, sweet girl, with all of our hearts."

Sydnee was officially three months old now, and we were preparing for our first trip to Boston Children's Hospital to meet the doctors in the Vascular Anomalies Center. This trip would be their opportunity to lay eyes on Sydnee and to give us a game plan for her treatment. They were the ones who knew the most about her syndrome, so this is where we needed to be. It was going to be a quick two day trip, but we were hopeful we would get some answers to our questions or be told new information that we needed to hear to best care for our daughter. The night before we flew out, we went to church as normal. It was there that our pastor and church friends surrounded us in a circle for prayer. It was such an amazing thing to experience. We already knew how much our church family loved and prayed for us, but this was just another reminder to stick in our minds as we faced the next two days. They each took turns praying out loud for us and for Sydnee, the doctors, and everyone involved. It gave us such a peace and comforting feeling that stuck with us for some time.

We made it safely to Boston and were anxious to meet the physicians. There they proceeded to take many pictures of Sydnee's body to have another document of who she was and how involved her syndrome was. We had already experienced this before at the pediatric surgeons' office back home, but it was still tough to undress her and let someone take many pictures of her physical limitations. They were very professional about their job, though, which made it easier to handle. Dr. Fishman came in with his nurse practitioners, Erin and Marybeth. The ladies commented right off the bat about Sydnee's hair bow. My little girls are known for their hair bows! They both were very friendly and easy-going. He felt like we should try to meet with the orthopedic surgeon while we were here, so he called for him to come to meet us. Dr. Kasser later walked into the room and went right to work. He took a look at Sydnee and then asked us several questions about her birth and such. He thought her hips looked and felt a little wide, so he sent us to have an ultrasound while he looked over her prenatal studies and records. Once we were back together, he confirmed that her right hip was definitely out of socket and the left one kept popping in and out. We were so disappointed! This condition can certainly happen to anyone, but why her, why did she need something else on her plate to deal with? Our plan was to follow up with someone local to fix her hips, and then he delivered the heavy news. Her hips would need to be corrected first and then her feet. In order to get her into a more normal shoe, he recommended removing a wedge or pizza slice-shaped section from her left foot and possibly a toe or two to make the foot narrower.

He continued that the same procedure could be attempted on the right foot, but that amputation was—in his opinion—the best option to give her the most function. At that moment, it felt like all of the air had been sucked out of the room! I was taken off guard by that news. I knew that was an option, but I just didn't expect to hear it today. All along, I had prayed that if Sydnee needed to have an amputation that God would just somehow take care of it in utero and not make Scott or myself make the decision. It is an irreversible decision, and what a big one to put on us! I guess I had somehow in my little mind concluded that if God had formed her this way, then this was how He wanted her to be…two big feet and all. It was all we could do to pay attention to the final moments of the consult. All we wanted to do at that moment was to get out of there as fast as we could so we could fall apart somewhere else besides this big hospital. That moment came as soon as we walked into our hotel room later. It was a rough evening, and we would have to recount all of it again as we called our families back home.

Exactly ten days after this first Boston trip and consult, we found ourselves in Dr. Madigan's office in Knoxville, closer to home. He was the pediatric orthopedist they referred us to and the closest one to our house. After another ultrasound, he also confirmed that Sydnee's right hip was definitely out of socket and the left one could pop in and out of place. He said that she would need to have surgery on both hips to correct them and then would be placed in a full-body cast for two to three months. I was taken aback and full of questions all at the same time. I couldn't believe she would have to deal with this on top of everything else unrelated to her syndrome. Why would God let all of this happen to my little girl? She was so young and innocent. It was in times like this that I wanted to scoop her up into my arms and run away from everyone and everything. As if that could do anything. It just seemed to blow my mind that in a few short weeks she would need surgery.

November 2nd came quickly. Sydnee was exactly four months old the date of her first surgery. We spent the morning doing preoperative exams and ultrasounds before registering at East Tennessee Children's Hospital. We dressed Sydnee in her hospital gown and held her so tightly. I hadn't slept very well in several nights, and I was so exhausted. Sydnee fell asleep while we waited for them to come for her. We carried her to the surgery doors and handed her over to the nurse. It was so hard to hand her over, but the fact that she was asleep made it a little easier for me, I think. After an hour or so in surgery, they told us she was going to get a CT scan to check on her hips before they let her wake up from surgery. We went to see her in recovery where we learned that the right hip had popped back out of place while they were placing her in the cast. She would need another surgery, and it was going to take place before the day was over. They cut the first cast off of her and took her back to surgery for a second round of anesthesia in the same day. By the end of this surgery, they told us they would have to wait until tomorrow to get the CT scan results read, and we wouldn't know until then if this second surgery was successful. She was, however, free to be discharged to go home tonight. We decided we should stay close to the hospital just in case, so we stayed in a hotel. Because Sydnee's cast went from her chest to her toenails, we needed to purchase bigger diapers, prop her onto her sides and get used to log rolling her so that she wouldn't get too uncomfortable in her cast. Fitting her into her car seat was the biggest problem. She, of course, wasn't going to fit into the infant carrier seat, so we had to purchase a new car seat. We used towels and blankets to prop her and help position her into the car seat so that she was safe to travel.

The nurses told us that her cast would only weigh 3-5 pounds, but once I picked her up, it felt like she had gained 20 pounds. I guess it was from the position she was placed into the cast. Her legs were split apart to make the angle better for the hips to strengthen into place. We couldn't pick her up under her arms like you would most babies this age. We had to put one hand on her upper body and the other one on her bottom to help support the weight of the cast and also prevent her from slipping out of the cast. We spent the first few days very close to home getting used to this new routine. By Sunday, Kerri and I needed to get out of the house. Knowing we desperately wanted to go to church, Scott came up with a plan to take our red wagon along with all of the extra throw pillows and blankets we used at home to make a traveling bed of sorts for Sydnee to go to church. When we arrived, we wheeled her inside, and everyone loved the idea. It was the best thing we could do to let her lie flat as well as move her comfortably. Big sister Kerri loved pulling Sydnee around in the red wagon all over the church. We were learning quickly that we would have to be creative with Sydnee's care. Whatever it took, we were determined to figure it out. God was close by and comforting us as only He can.

Two weeks later, we went back to Dr. Madigan for a follow up and another CT scan to recheck the hip placements. He said as far as he could tell, she looked great and that unfortunately their CT scanner was out of commission. We scheduled another CT at our local hospital and had plans to mail a disk of the scan back to him to evaluate. We would learn over Thanksgiving weekend that her right hip had in fact popped back out. She would need a third surgery to correct it and the three and a half weeks we had already been in the cast would have to be repeated. The left hip however, was still in place, thank the Lord. Dr. Madigan suggested we get the cast taken off until surgery to let her move around and her skin breathe a little before her next surgery. I was so excited for the day to get to snuggle with my youngest baby girl again.

The third hip surgery was scheduled for December 13, 2006. We met with Dr. Madigan the day before for a pre-op appointment. He expressed his doubts about this surgery working this time. He wanted to try again because it was so important to her mobility. He had already told us that because the right hip was so bad, she would probably need to have hip replacement surgery sometime in her thirties. Scott nor I slept much in the hotel the night before the procedure. Were we making the right decision? Why would we put her through another surgery if even the surgeon was doubtful about the outcome? We simply had to go on faith that this was the direction the Lord was guiding us. We had to at least try one more time to correct this hip.

Sydnee came through this surgery fine, and the initial CT scan showed that both hips were still in place. Sydnee, once again, had a hot pink full-body cast. This time, however, she was a lot more puffy and swollen in her face to the point that her eyes were almost forced shut. She was also in much more pain this time around. She cried most of the night in the hospital because she wanted me to hold her. She wasn't allowed to move much other than to change her diaper. We needed to make sure this hip stayed in place. As long as we kept her pain medicine coming, she was able to sleep. By the next morning, she was much better and seemed more relaxed and able to rest better.

By the two week follow-up appointment and CT scan, Dr. Madigan had good news for us: both hips still looked good. Finally, something was going right for my sweet girl! It felt like we were making progress and moving in the right direction.

The end of January 2007 finally came and we were back at Dr. Madigan's office to have the spica (body) cast removed. It was an exciting day for all of us. I wanted to hold my baby girl so close and I know she probably needed it too. It had only been six weeks, but Dr. Madigan felt like it was safe to remove the cast and use a hip brace. Once the cast was removed, we had to go down the hallway for an X-ray to check the angles of the hips. While I walked down the hall with Sydnee in my arms, she started kicking her left leg a little. The look on her face said it all. She smiled and started swinging both legs back and forth like she had just been freed! It was a priceless moment for me. God was so good!

We had to wait a few minutes until it was our turn, and while we were waiting, Sydnee started to jabber and swing her legs while sitting on my lap. It was almost as if she were trying to say, "Hey, everybody, look what I can do!" The X-rays were perfect and we were sent to the prosthestist, Mr. Karl. He had already made a custom pink brace for Sydnee. It took a while to be fitted just for her size, but after that, we were on our way home. It felt so good to hold my baby girl so close again. To actually feel my hands on her little back and her legs wrapped around me. It had been so long since I had felt this little "peanut." Once again, our hearts were so full. We were moving on from this hip problem and closer to being able to work on her feet so that she could walk someday. All along the way, God had been so close and so real. We may not have liked any part of it, but there was always a peace about the decisions we had to make for her. He was in control, and He was guiding us in the way we should go.

Chapter 7

UNEXPECTED NEWS

We were still getting used to Sydnee being out of her cast and in a brace. She wore this brace 24 hours a day over her clothes. She was only allowed to be out of it for diaper changes, bath, and changing clothes. She learned to roll over in it and even tried to sit up with it on. Because of the angles of the hips now, it was still a little difficult for her to sit up perfectly. We continued to get great news that her hips were staying in place and the angles of her hips were decreasing which was a good thing. Our cardiology appointments were going well also. Sydnee still had the ASD, but it wasn't affecting her overall growth and development. We had been sent to have tests performed to see the function of her kidneys. When those came back, the function was great, but they thought they saw a kidney stone on her left kidney. Because of this, we were now sent to a pediatric urologist. Yet another doctor.

We were definitely worried and didn't really know what to expect. If she did have a kidney stone, I wasn't sure how we would treat it. We would have to wait and see. Dr. Smith did the ultrasound himself and said she did not have a kidney stone. It was just a crazy case of hydronephrosis in the left kidney. We were momentarily relieved because we already knew that. She was doing okay with it so far, so he said we would continue to watch it. He also wanted to look at the right kidney because he thought he saw a mass there. Dr. Smith began to talk about the possibilities of what this could be. The short list of possibilities was a fluid-like pocket—another manifestation of her syndrome—or a Wilms tumor. Based on his experience, he felt pretty strongly that it was a cancer of the kidneys. I thought he must have been off his rocker! How could he know for sure that this was a cancerous tumor simply by looking at it on an ultrasound? Didn't he need a biopsy or something for confirmation? He talked for a while about what the next steps to take were. I don't remember much of the rest of the appointment I just wanted to get out of that office as fast as I could. Dr. Smith scheduled her to have a CT scan with and without contrast, but the soonest we could get it was one month away! How were we supposed to deal with this new information until then? Our car ride home was very quiet. Scott and I both were trying to process how this could be happening? We knew we would have to call our families and let them know, but we weren't really certain about what was going on. We didn't have a plan yet--we were just waiting for the CT scan. We decided the best thing was to tell our families that they did see a spot they wanted to check out again with a CT scan in about a month. It was the truth; we just couldn't "go there" and suggest she could possibly have cancer and worry them as well. For now, we kept the possible Wilms part to ourselves.

Journal entry from April 24, 2007:

I have to admit, I am very low right now with all of this uncertainty, but I know that God has a plan for your young life, and we're trusting in Him. He has all of the answers and already knows the outcome! I am trying to learn to depend on Him more and more every day. I love you, sweet girl!

After the CT scan and X-rays, Dr. Smith concluded that the mass was most likely a Wilms tumor as he had thought. He told us our two options were to remove the entire kidney or biopsy the mass in the kidney and risk spilling the contents into the abdomen. We were so worried and confused. How could we make the choice to remove her kidney when she was eleven months old? It was a huge, irreversible decision. Wilms tumors were very treatable if it was cancer. However, if we did only the biopsy and found out later it was Wilms, then we could have done more damage and perhaps spread the cancer across her belly. Dr. Smith told us he would suggest to remove the kidney just to be on the safe side, but it was definitely our decision to make. He suggested that whatever we decided be done soon.

We left his office and headed home to pray about what God would have us do. How do you make that kind of decision as a parent? It would definitely be a tough one. The mass was located in her right kidney which was the pretty one. The left kidney was the one with hydronephrosis and looked "funky," as Dr. Smith called it. We knew the function was good, but for how long? What if we removed the only "good" kidney and then the left one gave out at some point? If we only biopsied the mass and it was cancer, then we made the wrong decision. On the other hand, if we removed the right kidney and it was benign, then was that the wrong decision? I just remember having that rain cloud feeling again like when I was pregnant with Sydnee. I wanted so desperately to make the right decision, or not make a decision at all. If I could have, I would have taken it for her.

A few days passed and Scott and I both were still confused and scared as ever. We had researched as much as we could and even called her physicians in Boston to get their opinions. One evening after giving the girls a bath, we each took one to dress. Scott had Sydnee and was blowing on her belly to get her to laugh. He heard a voice say, "Don't worry about the kidney. It will be fine." He was shocked and tried to ask which kidney He was talking about. If it was the right one, then maybe that was our answer. If it was the left one, we weren't so sure. The days were dwindling away; we needed to make a decision. Somehow, we both felt like we should remove the right kidney just in case the biopsy came back positive for cancer. It was the best way to lessen the risk and give her the best outcome.

So, on June 14, 2007 at eleven months old, Sydnee was taken into surgery to remove her right kidney. She tolerated the procedure very well and actually recovered quickly. A few days later, some of the pathology report had come back to say the mass was in fact a Wilms tumor and it was cancer. Because we caught it, she wouldn't need chemotherapy. What a relief--we had made the right decision! Dr. Smith did tell us that there were more pathology reports pending and it would take a few days until it all came back, but for now, it looked okay. Three days later, Scott received a phone call at work that changed our worlds yet again. The final path reports had come back, and it looked like Sydnee's tumor was a Stage 2 Wilms tumor. Without lymph nodes to sample, which would verify if they got it all, we would need to have chemotherapy. I was blown away when he told me this. My eleven-month-old would need to have chemotherapy because she had cancer that was inside of her.

Scott called the head of the cancer board at the time and spoke with her directly for advice. Some doctors were telling us they should have gotten everything and wouldn't need chemo while others recommended chemo to be sure and give her the greatest chance at a long life. Again, we were sent to several doctors to talk about what types of chemotherapy Sydnee would need and what schedule she would take. All this time, my head was spinning. I couldn't believe this baby girl was going to face something this big again.

Sydnee would need a porta-cath placed

under her skin so that she could receive her chemotherapy and not have to be stuck with an IV catheter each time. This meant she would have yet another surgery for the device placement. It was uncanny to me that this would be her fifth surgery in eight months! I knew underneath all of this, that God was in control and that He knew about everything that was going on with Sydnee; I just wasn't too happy about it. He didn't ask me, after all. I wasn't sure how this ride was going to go. I just knew all I could do was to pray for her and to seek God's will in all circumstances.

Sydnee turned one year old on July 2, 2007, and started chemotherapy one week later on July 9. She had to have surgery for the porta-cath placement as well as nasogastric (NG) tube (a tube from the nose to the stomach) for feedings. In all of our meetings with the hematology oncologists, they told us she would need to have a tube feeding all night long of Pediasure for extra calories because she was so tiny. The chemo could suppress her appetite and these extra calories would help sustain her weight. We were the most comfortable with the hospital in Knoxville since we had used them for her hip surgeries. Because of this, we decided to drive her there for all of her treatments. It was a sacrifice, but one that we felt God would help us maintain. This was where we thought we should be to keep tabs on her hips as well as her kidney. Her chemotherapy routine would be once a week every week for the first ten weeks and then once every three weeks after that for a total of nineteen weeks. The morning of the port placement, both Scott and I were so worried. In spite of all of our nerves and fears, there was an underlying peace in the situation. It was completely out of our control, but at the same time, that was okay too. We had enough to worry about, and God was somehow showing us His presence in an uncomfortable situation.

The surgeon came out and told us that the catheter was in place and he used the smallest one he had, but he still wasn't sure it would stay under her skin. Due to her small size, he was afraid it might come back out.

From there, we waited until she woke up from surgery before they would give her the chemotherapy. Receiving the chemo didn't take that long. It was a slow IV push instead of a drip. She was getting such a small dose it seemed to go quickly. As soon as we were discharged from the hospital, we scooted over to see Dr. Madigan for a hip X-ray and follow-up. There he told us he was concerned about the angles of her hips. He wanted her to wear the hip brace during nap and bedtimes and would need to see her again in three more months. For now, that was on the back burner. My concern was just getting her home without her getting sick from the chemotherapy. We met with home health to get the medical equipment needed for me to maintain her NG tube as well as to manage her tube feedings each night. Sydnee would pull her NG tube out of her nose whether by accident or on purpose, but by bedtime it would have to go back in for sure. Sometimes, Scott had to work late and wouldn't be home in time to help me place the tube again. I had to incorporate Kerri into the procedure and let her be my helper or second pair of hands. At three years old, Kerri would gently hold Sydnee's head to the side so that I could insert the tube and then tape it before checking it. I would sit on the floor with my legs extended and put Sydnee on the floor between my legs with her tiny hands under my legs to keep them out of the way. Kerri was always ready to help and would say soothing things to Sydnee like, "It's okay; we're almost finished." It was the sweetest thing to see, but also a much needed helper to me. The struggle was to find the time to put her to bed so that she would be able to sleep the entire time that the feeding infused. She was a very good sleeper, but she hadn't been waking up during the night to eat in such a long time. I wasn't sure how she would tolerate a full stomach all night long as well as a tube taped to her face.

For the most part, we were making it pretty well each week with her chemotherapy. I could certainly tell a decrease in her appetite overall especially for the first two days after chemo. It was on these days that she might eat a couple of saltine crackers all day long along with breast milk. I was so worried about her weight gain and overall nutrition. By week three of chemotherapy, I began to notice that Sydnee's hair was beginning to come out slowly. I was so worried about this part. This was where she would start to look sick with the hair loss and the NG tube on her face. Since it was still summer and the weather was nice, we were still able to take her out in public to places that weren't too crowded and where people wouldn't be able to touch her. How would they react to seeing her? We were already somewhat used to getting looks and stares from others when we were out in public. This was just something extra for them to look at. It was tough to deal with as her mommy, but in no way as tough as it was on her little body, I am sure. My little girls always wear a hair bow in their hair even when we are just playing at home. I would still put the bow in her hair; I was just extra careful when brushing it now. We were already looking for hats to wear the rest of this season and some for the winter, but for now, we had to get a little creative in the accessory department. When both girls were newborns, we used a water based lubricant to help little ribbon bows stick to their heads. Now that her hair was starting to come out, we started using a little bit bigger bow and adhering it to her head. Problem solved.

By week four of chemotherapy, Sydnee's blood counts were too low for her to receive both chemotherapy agents. Since one of them affected the blood count, she had to hold off on that one. It would make for an easier week for Sydnee with the nausea, but it would also extend her chemo one more week. We knew going into it that extensions could happen; it was just crazy that we were seeing side effects so soon in treatment.

I wait for the LORD, my whole being waits, and in His word I put my hope.

Psalm 130:5

Each year in the first two weeks of August,

we tried to attend a few days of Nazarene district meetings and church camp back home in West Virginia. We knew we couldn't stay both weeks, but a few days would be better than nothing. After all, this was our normal routine, and we were trying to do things as a family as close to normal as possible. Since Sydnee was taking chemotherapy, we knew her immune system was being compromised. We would need to be extra careful this week around our friends and family. We figured if we came to the services late, sat off to the side by ourselves, and left early we would be okay. We had them announce this from the platform so that people would respect our chance of getting out without getting too close to make her sick. They were so wonderful and kind and kept their distances the whole time we were there.

It was great seeing old friends and meeting new ones. After several days of being there, my dad had mentioned to Scott and me that many, many people wanted to hear from us on how we were doing. My dad thought it was a good idea to bring Sydnee up on the platform during the service to let the camera show her in a close-up on the screen. We talked it over and agreed. This was the best way, we thought, to let everyone see her sweet face and smile without getting too close. In the next service, we went on stage to show Sydnee off, and boy, did she smile under her pretty pink and white flowered hat! She was becoming quite the ham for the camera these days! Scott began to give a short update on her progress and shared a little of our testimony and how the Lord was providing and sustaining us these days.

When we sat down, someone sent a note to the platform that they thought the congregation should take a love offering for our family. We were shocked and honestly embarrassed at first. We were doing okay financially. It wasn't cheap to drive two hours one way every week for chemotherapy, pay out of pocket for tube feedings and anti-nausea medication, but God was faithful and He would work it out. We sat there in that service as they collected an offering and then said they would continue to collect money for the rest of the week as long as it was marked with our name. Each service after that one, we heard people testify how they felt led to give sacrificially to our family. Some gave their food money for the rest of the day when they didn't know how they would find money for food to eat. That same person said someone else came to them and gave them money back that they had owed them and the original person had long forgotten about the money. There were similar stories told where the Lord had laid us on their hearts and told them to give money and then somehow, their needs were met also. All Scott and I could do was sit there and let the tears fall on our faces. How humbling!

One evening after service, I talked with my dad and told him that they needed to stop giving money. The campground could use this money, we were okay for now and that was enough. I was feeling pretty awful about this. I told him we could turn around and put the money back in the offering plates and give it to the camp. He told me that the

Lord had laid this on someone's heart and that they were obeying God by giving as He led the people to give. In his opinion, God knew much better than we did at the moment (or any moment for that matter) and we needed to openly accept the offering. This was what God would want us to do. By the end of the week, the offering had come to be $7500! What a blessing!

We came home the next day to find several hospital bills due at the same time. God was so good! His ways are best!

Call to me and I will answer you and tell you great and unsearchable things you do not know.

Jeremiah 33:3

Journal entry August 12, 2007

Sydnee, God knows exactly what you need when you need it! May you always remember these times of how God always provides at just the right time. May you always be willing to share your testimony of God's grace in your life. I love you and am praying for you!

After returning home from church camp, both Scott and I continued to struggle with accepting the very generous love offering. Yes, we were now receiving medical bills, but they were manageable for now, and we felt so unworthy. One day while Scott was on his way home from work, he came to a stoplight. It was there that God told him, "Stop worrying about the money. It's not about the money. I've given you Sydnee to raise, but I want you to know you are not doing it alone." He said he couldn't get home fast enough to tell me all about it. From that day on, we decided that God must have a bigger plan for her than we could ever imagine. For now, we felt it was best to save that money for her when she was older or when the need was greater.

While we were home this week, we had more chemotherapy and a cardiac appointment. Dr. Madhok said, "Unfortunately her ASD hasn't closed up any, but the good news is that you are otherwise doing well despite everything." I had secretly hoped it would have closed up so that we would have one less thing to deal with. Oh, well, we are still confident that God is in control and that He knows best. Until then, we will continue to watch everything and trust in His plan for our lives.

By the weekend, Scott had gone out of town, and my mom was able to come down to spend the weekend with me and the girls. I was so thankful for her extra set of hands. Sunday morning we got up and were getting dressed and ready for church. We noticed that Sydnee felt a little warm, so I checked her temperature. In her bottom it was 104, and in her ear it was 102.6. My mom put her into the bathtub to cool her off while I called the pediatrician. He said we needed to get her to the hospital to check her out and that he would meet us in the pediatric unit.

After drawing blood and urine, Dr. Shook wanted to admit her for a few days to see if the cultures grew anything. By the next morning,

Sydnee's iron level reading had come back--too low. She had to have a blood infusion to bring it back up. By Wednesday, the blood cultures had come back to show that she was septic. We knew this could happen, I was just hoping it would not. She would need to be on antibiotics for a total of ten days and since they were using her central line for access instead of an IV, our pediatrician didn't feel comfortable sending us home. It meant we were in the hospital for the long haul. While we were there, we couldn't have any visitors other than grandparents and us. Needless to say, the days grew very long. When someone would leave the room, whether it was family or medical staff, Sydnee would cry. She wanted to get out of that room as much as I did. All the nurses were so taken with her. They would bring her special toys and books from the playroom to occupy her. One of them even made her a personal name tag on a pull cord just like the nurses. Every time one of them came into her room to check her vitals, Sydnee would grab their nametag and play with it while they were in our room. It didn't matter what hospital we were in—either outpatient or inpatient—Sydnee had a way of winning over hearts.

By Friday, we had talked Dr. Shook into letting us go home and let me and home health maintain the antibiotics at home. By the afternoon, we were getting ready to go home and I thought she felt warm. We checked her temperature and sure enough, she had a fever. We were stuck here a few more days. By Monday morning—day eight—Dr. Shook came in early to take a look at Sydnee's port and noticed that some of it was sticking out of her skin. Her skin was so tight that it somehow had worked it out. I was so bummed. We were finally getting to leave the hospital room, but it wasn't for home, it was for an ambulance ride to the Children's Hospital in Knoxville, almost two hours away! As we left on the stretcher later that morning, all of the nurses lined the hallway and told Sydnee goodbye. They waved and blew kisses to her like she was royalty. That was the effect everywhere we went. My sweet Sydnee had stolen their hearts in a matter of a few days.

By 2:00 pm that afternoon Sydnee was in surgery to remove the porta-cath. Yes, chemo-therapy would have to be extended yet again. We spent the night in the hospital there alone and then were discharged home with home health to come and manage the remainder of IV antibiotics. Once home, she was so happy to be with Kerri again and to play with her own toys. I had noticed that her appetite was much better since we had stopped the chemotherapy.

One week later, we were back in Knoxville for another surgery to place another central line called a Broviac. I would have to do sterile dressing changes at home and flush the line once a day for the remainder of her chemotherapy. I had exper-ience doing this, but having to do this on my own child was a different ballgame. However, if she had needed me to walk to the moon, I would have. As a parent, that's just what you do for your children. We also restarted the chemotherapy treatments. It was now the beginning of September, and if we didn't have any more delays, we would have to have chemotherapy until Christmas.

By the next week, we had a post-op follow-up appointment with Dr. Shook to check her blood counts. Her platelet count was way too low. Needless to say, chemotherapy was postponed yet again, and we were stuck back in the hospital. The nurses were all happy to see us. This time, Sydnee was feeling much better and was ready to play. We placed blankets on the floor of the hospital room. I know there is a certain *ick* factor with that, but when your fourteen-month-old wants to play on the floor, you do whatever is necessary. She sat there with her shiny bald head and wore her pearl necklaces. It was such a small thing, but to her, it was what brought a smile to her face. She just needed to get out of that hospital bed. Two days later, her platelets were up some, but not enough. Dr. Shook contacted the cancer doctors as well as the doctors in Boston, and they all concluded that Sydnee had a condition called ITP (idiopathic thrombocytopenic purpura, a condition involving a very low platelet count). This was probably due to her chemotherapy. We were able to go home the next day, but we would have to be very careful.

By Thanksgiving, we felt like it was time to start keeping Sydnee home even more. We couldn't have her around the public very much because of the risk of catching something while her immune system was so depressed. We couldn't let anyone in our house or near her who didn't have a flu shot. As a result of this, I wasn't sure how I was going to be able to let Kerri stay in dance class every week. If I couldn't have Sydnee around other people, then how could I take Kerri to class? I asked one lady from my church, Mrs. Barbara, if she could help me out some. She agreed and was willing to get the flu shot just so that she could sit with Sydnee in the house while Kerri and I were in dance class. It wasn't just her either—I had several people in the church who didn't ordinarily get the flu shot but were now willing to take it for Sydnee and Kerri too. I felt so bad asking them for their help, but they were excited to be able to help out. It was such a blessing to me, not only to know how many people loved us, but also to have this special time alone with Kerri each week. The Lord is so good and faithful. His mercies are new every morning!

Because of the LORD's great love we are not consumed, for His compassions never fail. They are new every morning; great is your faithfulness.
                                           Lamentations 3:22-23

Up until now, Scott and Kerri would go to Sunday school and church at the normal times. With cold and flu season starting in full swing, we knew we needed to be more careful. Sydnee and I would stay at home from church while Scott and Kerri would go. I would then take Kerri back to church on Sunday nights and Wednesday nights myself while Scott and Sydnee stayed home. Poor Sydnee, I think she was getting just as bored being at home all of the time just like I was. The only time she left the house was for a doctor's appointment or more chemotherapy. I can remember getting the girls to bed at night and then running off to Wal-Mart by myself just to get out of the house or to run my errands at 9:00 at night. It was a crazy time in our lives, but it was what was necessary to keep our baby girl as protected and healthy as we could.

December 27, 2007 was a special day for our whole family, because it was Sydnee's last chemotherapy appointment! We had waited and longed for this day for what seemed like forever. She started the chemo in July and was just now finishing. Through it all, God kept her safe and healthy for the most part. We almost skipped our way to the chemo clinic that day! Perhaps the best way to describe my thoughts and feelings is to share my journal entry for that day with you.

Journal entry Thursday, December 27, 2007

Sydnee, today we drove to Knoxville for your very last chemotherapy dosage and abdominal ultrasound. We have waited so long for this day, sweet girl. I cannot believe you have been receiving treatments for over five months now. You are such a trooper and have come through this chemotherapy very well in my eyes. I know that God has kept His hand over you during this time to keep you healthy. When we first found out that you would need chemo treatments, it seemed as though it would be an impossible mountain to climb. However, your journey is a testimony to God's grace and wisdom. You see, had you not had the hydronephrosis in your left kidney at birth, we wouldn't have been getting abdominal ultrasounds and found the tumor in your right kidney. Since we caught the tumor so early, it may have saved you from suffering a lot of pain if it had gone longer and grown bigger. Even though I've always known it in my head, God will always give you what you need at only the exact time that you need it! Now, I know it in my heart and will never doubt or forget it! God has a wonderful and unique plan for your life, sweet girl. May you always grow to know what He has done for you and perhaps through you. It is my prayer that you will always remain close to God and allow Him to use you in any way He desires. I am so thankful for today and so proud of you. My heart is so full! Love, your grateful mommy

Wait for the LORD; be strong and take heart and wait for the LORD.

Psalm 27:14

A few weeks later, our lives were still just as busy and we had a full day ahead of us with post-chemotherapy blood work, removal of the central line (Broviac catheter), and a hip X-ray and follow-up. We didn't like scheduling the days this busy, but when all of the appointments are so far away, we tried to get them all over with as closely as we could. To accurately recount this day, I have included a portion of the e-mail that I shared with our friends that day, January 14, 2008:

We left our house at 6:00 am to be there for blood work at 8:00 am and then to have her Broviac taken out. The blood work came back a little low, but okay. The surgeon decided he wanted to use some sedation to remove the central line, which meant she had to be NPO (nothing by mouth) for at least eight hours prior. When Scott called to confirm the appointment last week, they told him she could eat before this appointment, so we had fed her before we left our house. Needless to say, we had a lot of time to kill on our hands before the 1:20 pm appointment time with the orthopedist. We decided to take her to the mall since it was cold. We basically walked around aimlessly in the dumps because we knew that our day hadn't started out well and that was probably how the events would run this afternoon with the orthopedist.

We were in one store and a young couple with a baby came up behind us and started small talk with us (general things like what was Sydnee's name, how old she was, did we have any other children, and so on). Of course, we asked the same general questions in return. Then, the man looked at us and said that at his church, they had been studying how to be a bolder Christian. He said they had talked about if you see someone whom you felt needed prayer to pray for them right there. He then asked us if he could pray with us. We looked at each other and then agreed. He went on to ask us if there was anything specifically we wanted him to pray for. I looked at Scott as if to say, "Where do we begin?" and, "Sir, you don't have enough time for us to list everything."

Scott simply said we have an appointment this afternoon that is very important. He took those words from Scott and then started to pray the most beautiful and appropriate prayer for us and Sydnee. He said things like, "I pray that they would leave the doctor with joyful hearts at the news they received and may they know that God has healed their daughter." I cannot type fast enough or say enough to you to express how perfect his prayer was.

He basically just encouraged us instead of telling us anything new. But, he did say that he felt that he was at the mall to buy a rug and to pray with us! Scott and I didn't know what to say other than a tearful thank you.

Sometimes, your heart gets so heavy that you just can't pray for yourself or your own needs. It's just great to know that there are others out there that can heed the presence of the Lord in their lives and pray for us. We don't even know that man's name or much else about him. However, I feel as though it was God speaking to us through him.

We finally went to see the orthopedist, and he said Sydnee does not need to have hip surgery! The angles of her hip alignment had decreased in the last three months to an acceptable range. He cleared us to go to Boston and begin work there on her feet. I have always felt that God could heal Sydnee completely if He so chose. I just didn't think that was what He had in store for her. I don't know…I certainly don't have all of the answers, but I feel like yesterday was a huge day for our family. I feel as though it confirmed to me that God did perform a miracle in Sydnee…He healed her hips! It doesn't always take much in life, just a grateful heart and a willing spirit. Thank you, thank you, thank you! There are no words to describe or demonstrate the joy in my heart. For now, we are resting. No doctor appointments are scheduled (other than well checks) for at least three months! Little is much when God is in it!

Let the morning bring me word of Your unfailing love, for I have put my trust in You.

Psalm 143:8

We were officially finished with chemotherapy and were seeing her blood counts rise again to more normal limits. Her appetite was also increasing. That was so exciting! We were slowly easing her back into the public. We still wanted to be so careful but were so ready to show her off. We planned a "No More Chemo" party for her and for our family and friends as a way to say, "Here she is and thank you to everyone for all of your prayers!"

Chapter 8

BOSTON, HERE WE COME!

As soon as we had the green light to head to Boston to follow up with the Vascular Anomalies Center there, we started making plans for a trip. In the first week of April 2008, we headed up there to let everyone see Sydnee and fill them in a little on what we had been up to lately. They were all so very astonished to see her look so happy and healthy following everything she had been through. They hadn't seen her since she was three months old and couldn't get over how strong she was and how she scooted herself around dragging her right leg while using the left leg to scoot. It sounds weird, but this was the way she found to help her get from one place to another without having to crawl around everywhere. We called it her "modified walking."

We spent practically the entire day there with appointments, pictures, and exams to catch up. Dr. Kasser, the pediatric orthopedist, still said he felt the best approach to full mobility for Sydnee was to amputate the right foot below the knee. Along with this, we would need to come back in four months and remove two toes from her left foot (a wedge resection or pie-shaped portion) to make the left foot more narrow and more able to fit into a shoe. It was still difficult to hear and know that we would have to make these decisions for her, but somehow there was a peace about the whole situation.

Our summer was spent getting ready for Sydnee's surgery in Boston. Originally, we were scheduled for surgery in June, but it was rescheduled due to the doctor's schedule. This new surgery date would be September 4, 2008. They had told us to plan on staying in Boston at least two weeks for this surgery, so it meant a lot of planning to arrange our schedules and to arrange things like bill payments while we were gone. We drove to Charleston, West Virginia to spend the night with my parents before our flight on Monday from there. On Sunday, we noticed Sydnee was trying to take a few steps towards walking. She had to practically stand on her toes with her right foot and then straighten out her leg since it was longer than the left one. The next step with the left one was flat footed like normal, but a big step down. It was exciting to see, but also heartbreaking because here she was actually trying to do it all on her own, and we were days away from amputating the right foot. At the same time, it also confirmed to me that she was going to need some help. Maybe this was God's way of showing me that the amputation was necessary for her overall well-being. With the prosthesis it would be easier for her to walk. We could help her compensate for the leg length and let her stand up straight with both legs fully extended.

We flew out to Boston on Monday, Labor Day. By Tuesday, our schedule was changing yet again. All of the pre-op checks were looking great until we met with the cardiologist for cardiac clearance. After a long wait and more tests, they said they felt her ASD was still too large to take the risk of a big surgery like an amputation without first trying to address closure of the ASD. *What*? We were only here to get the okay for surgery. We had just signed the consent for the surgery a few hours earlier and now they were saying it might not even happen. It was a crazy afternoon and now evening. We had been at the hospital since 6:00 am for Sydnee's MRI and other pre-op appointments. We were there until 7:00 pm. Due to the type of surgery she was scheduled to have, they felt like it was too big a risk to let her heart go untouched. I guess with orthopedic surgery, the risk could have been higher for her to throw a blood clot.

We understood what they were saying and why it was just now a big deal as well as the urgency to attempt to fix it before such a big surgery. They wanted to be extra careful, so when we left the hospital that Tuesday evening, they told us she was scheduled for ASD closure the next morning and they would call us later that night to tell us what time to be at the hospital in the morning. By this point, we were beginning to think that every time we came to Boston, we were going to hear bad news. Later when they called us, they said she was going to be the second case the next morning.

Wednesday morning we woke up and were at the hospital waiting for Sydnee to be prepped and taken for the TEE (transesophageal echocardiogram), an ultrasound test that gives the best pictures of the heart, and possible ASD repair. They were finally ready to begin the test, and if it looked good, they would proceed on with the device repair.

They kept us very well-informed, and after about three hours they told us that they had secured a device to close the hole from the ASD. Everything moved pretty quickly after that. The nurse came back out to say the doctor would be out to talk with us. The doctor came right out and introduced himself as Dr. Lock. He took us back to the cath lab section and showed us her scans. I don't think most parents get to see this area. All of the nurses and techs were looking at us a little strangely. He said that her ASD (atrial septal defect) was larger than they had thought and that it took him five attempts to seat a device properly due to the size and shape of the defect. He said he used a device called a CardioSeal. He said it is the most difficult one to place, and most physicians don't like to use them for that reason. Dr. Lock said the device didn't fully close the hole, but what was left was a small part that shouldn't cause a problem.

Sydnee was doing great in recovery, and if all went well and the device stayed in place, then she could still have her amputation surgery the following morning as previously planned.

That evening we were hanging out in Sydnee's room on the cardiac floor and the nurses were all amazed at the fact that Dr. Lock had done her surgery. Not knowing much about him, we were a little taken aback by their questioning. Come to find out, this doctor who just happened to have time on his schedule for our special needs daughter was the top rated one as well as the one of the doctors who pioneered this procedure. Along with that, the resident who was also managing her care had done some training at Mayo Clinic and had worked with other Klippel-Trenaunay-Weber patients and their hearts. My friends, we serve an awesome God! He knew who needed to be where and at what time so that everything would work out. We didn't know it, but He sure did!

Thursday morning came very early for us. Sydnee had another EKG and cardiac ECHO that showed everything looked good. I was able to paint Sydnee's toenails on her right foot one more time before they came to take us to the holding area. I remember tears rolling down my cheeks as I painted her nails. It was the last time that I would ever have the chance to paint all ten of her toenails. I don't know why that was so important to me, but I just needed to do it. I think Sydnee knew something was going on because she wanted to be held a lot that morning. Our families had shown up and were able to spend some time with us before the surgery. Along with them, our good friend Shep surprised us and walked into her hospital room that morning! He had flown in the night before and wanted to be there a few days to support us! What an amazing friend! It was great to have so much support not only in person, but also back home.

I was a nervous wreck, but I knew God was

in control. Too many times before He has supplied our needs, and I knew He would take care of my little one today.

We were moved to the pre-op holding area where we met with the surgeon, Dr. Kasser, once again. He began to use a pen to draw a line on Sydnee's right leg and then signed his initials on her right foot. I knew what this meant. It bothered me because it bothered Sydnee. She whimpered and rubbed on her blanket while he finished talking with us.

I don't know why it mattered, but we asked Dr. Kasser if they ever used any of the amputated tissue for research. He said Dr. Fishman was conducting a study and they were currently accepting donations for a research project, and if we were interested, he could have someone from the research department come and talk with us. We agreed and looked forward to finding out more information.

It was finally time to take Sydnee back for surgery. Man, it was so tough letting her go. This time, she was two years old and much more aware of what was going on. She was scared and needed her mommy. We weren't able to take her back to the OR because they had a lot of people back in that area already. They told us the surgery should last somewhere between 2-4 hours after they had her sedated and an IV started. They would call us with updates while she was in surgery.

It was definitely hard to hand Sydnee over, but we knew we had to. She cried and said, "I need my mommy!" It broke my heart. If I could have, I would have taken this surgery for her, but it wasn't up to me. We had prayed and felt like this was the direction we should take to give her the best opportunity to walk, run, and move freely as she grew. As soon as we were in the waiting room, they called to say she had calmed down very quickly and that she was asleep (sedated) and they were ready to start.

While we were waiting to hear more from the surgery, a lady from the research team came to talk with us about donating Sydnee's tissue. It was a strange thing for me to do, but I felt like if her foot was no use to her currently, then maybe studying it may help someone else out or even Sydnee later on down the road. Again, there was a peace about this decision and one that made us feel that we were doing the right thing even if we were scared to death.

Four hours later, Dr. Kasser came out to talk with us and say the surgery was over, and Sydnee did very well. He said he still felt this was the best decision for her and that he thought she would do very well overall. How nice of him to offer us encouragement exactly when I needed some! I truly feel like God gives us exactly what we need at the precise moment we need it, not a moment before or after.

Sydnee did pretty well the next few days dealing with pain and trying to wake up from the pain medicine. They started out giving her morphine on a pain pump and it seemed like it kept her too sleepy. She would wake up to talk to us or to take a drink, and then before we knew it, she was back to sleep. When we were finally able to keep her awake long enough to eat something and keep it down, they switched her to oral pain medicine. She seemed to tolerate this much better and was able to stay awake to eat, play, and talk with us for longer periods of time. By three days post-op, Sydnee was able to be discharged from the hospital to our hotel. We needed to stay in town for a while to see how she was going to heal. It was hotel living, but we were all together in the same place. It was a small room, but we worked on puzzles, played card games, and watched movies. After a day or so, we were able to take Sydnee out around town using her stroller. She loved being outside just as much as we did. It was a great way to see Boston and to find some fun places to explore.

Tuesday morning, Sydnee woke up around 5:45 am and was hungry. She was now five days post-op and her appetite was returning. I tried to convince her to go back to sleep that it was too early to eat, but she wasn't having it. I got up out of bed to get her something quick—a Pop Tart, her favorite. When I came back to bed, she kept asking to "nuggle you" which meant she wanted me to snuggle with her in her bed. I climbed into bed with her and noticed something rough on my leg. I thought her right leg had fallen off of the pillow that we had placed in the bed to elevate her leg while she slept. I lifted the blankets to look for the cast but saw it safely positioned on the pillow. I further drew back the sheets to find her right leg free from the cast and moving all around the bed. Her entire cast had slid off in bed! I woke Scott up, and we called the doctor to ask what we needed to do. They told us to bring her back into the hospital so we could wrap the leg with an ace wrap to protect the incision until we arrived. We were able to get a sneak peak at her incision, and it looked really good. She was a little worried about it, and wanted me to "put it back on." I wasn't sure if she didn't like the sutures or if she noticed her foot was gone, or if she just needed her cast back on. Kerri wanted to take a look, so we showed it to her. She didn't say much and acted like that was the way her leg had always looked.

At the clinic, Dr. Kasser said her leg looked wonderful and that we could get her fitted for the prosthesis in about one month. They made a modified cast-like splint for her leg, and we were able to leave the hospital again. While we were downstairs in the lobby waiting for the taxi to pick us up, Sydnee started cruising around the chairs. It was a little crazy to me that she was able to take steps five days after surgery. Go figure. God was doing a mighty work in my little girl.

We had one more incision check before we were able to leave Boston and fly home. It had now been a full two weeks that we had been there, and we were all a little tired of being in a hotel. We finally made it back home to Tennessee and came home to such a wonderful welcome. Our friends had decorated our house and front yard with welcome home signs and lots of pink! Inside, we found a wonderful meal and lots of goodies for the girls. It was another reminder of what awesome friends we have and how much they loved our little girls.

We were home and adjusting to life after surgery. Sydnee was still learning that she couldn't get around as easily with a cast on her leg. Because of her limited mobility, they told us we needed to give her Lovenox injections twice a day for several weeks following surgery. This was to prevent clotting as she was going to be less mobile since she was now in a cast. It was tough for me being her mommy to have to give her a shot two times a day, but I thought it was easier for me to do it than to have a stranger do it in a doctor's office. Along with this, we had to wrap her leg twice a day with three elastic wraps with a splint to add compression and stability. She tolerated the shots and the dressing changes pretty well. She didn't like to see the incision and would cry often saying, "Mommy, no lady bugs." I think she thought the sutures were lady bugs. Once I had her first ace wrap on her leg, she was fine and the tears would stop. After a week or so, I guess she adjusted to the routine and tried to help me tear the tape for her ace wraps. I had always included big sister Kerri in her care, so she liked to re-roll the ace wraps when I would take them off. It was a small thing, but in some way, I think she felt so important and loved to help out her little sister.

We ended up having to give Sydnee the Lovenox injections for three weeks following the surgery. The day finally came when we gave the last shot. Sydnee quickly learned the expression "No more shots!" For several days after the last shot, she would say, "Mommy, no more shots." We, of course, had to have a little party complete with cookies to celebrate such a big day! Sydnee's follow up appointments with the orthopedist and cardiologist went very well. She was healing well and looking good. Our God is a great big God, but He's never too busy to take care of the little things too!

Chapter 9

WALKING

We started physical therapy again with Sydnee three weeks after surgery. She was ready to do new things, and she wanted to move. Mrs. Jill was our therapist, and that made Sydnee very happy. Mrs. Jill has lots of fun toys in her room, and that was a huge deal to this little girl. By the end of the appointment, Mrs. Jill wanted to see what Sydnee could do with a walker. She was looking at how well she stayed balanced and how quickly she would be able to walk independently. She placed her behind the forward moving walker and Sydnee took right to it! She was so excited to get to use the "stroller" as she called it. She walked the whole length of the hallway behind it and wanted to go farther, but it was time for us to leave. Jill thought it wouldn't be long before she was walking upright independently. How I longed for that day!

Over the next few days, I had begun to watch Sydnee walk behind her doll strollers more often; the only problem was that she was leaning too heavily on such a lightweight object that she often almost turned it over with her. By the beginning of October, we were at home on a normal day cleaning and doing laundry. I came into the room to see what the girls were up to and noticed Sydnee was taking a few steps all on her own. She wasn't holding onto a toy or Kerri, but standing by herself in the middle of the room. All along, I had dreamed of the day my two-year-old would walk independently and here it was. I was watching it first hand, and then it dawned on me that I needed to get the video camera to catch this memory. The strange thing about her walking was that it seemed so natural for her. She was smiling and so proud of herself. This was different. She was standing more upright and less bent as she had been previously. She was doing it, and it looked wonderful. I know for her it must have felt so good to finally be able to get where she wanted to go without holding onto something or someone or having to crawl on the floor like a baby.

About one week later, we had to go to another therapy session and then would leave from there to head back to Knoxville for doctors' appointments. While we were at therapy, Sydnee had a great time until it was just about ready to be over. Mrs. Jill wanted Sydnee to walk with the walker one more time to help with her stability. Sydnee was getting hungry and was eying the M&Ms in her bag. She kept asking for them and I tried to quietly convince her to finish therapy and we could have those later. She wanted no part of being denied her favorite snack of M-Mies as she called them. She sat down on the mat and began to cry and throw the biggest fit. I was mortified to say the least. Needless to say, the therapy session was over and we were quickly out the door.

My mom was down with us and had kept Kerri while we went to therapy. Once we picked them up at home, my mom asked Sydnee what she did at therapy today. Sydnee told her about playing with the balls and the marble game in the tube. Nana asked her if she walked with the "stroller" today, and Sydnee said no. Nana asked why not? To which Sydnee replied, "I frew (threw) a fit." She then smiled from ear to ear. Such an ornery little thing! That was my Sydnee. She had so much to deal with in life I guess having a big personality to go along with it helped.

On that same day, after therapy, we headed down to Knoxville for a chemo follow up appointment as well as the first measurements for the prosthesis. It was going to be a full day, but we had to squeeze everything in. The check-up went well and we were off to meet with Mr. Karl for the prosthesis. Sydnee was a little unsure of what we were going to do here, so when we sat her on the table and began to unwrap the ace wraps on her leg, she didn't want to stay there. Mr. Karl needed to get some measurements of her leg and used a sharpie pen to mark her landmarks around her knee. Sydnee was so scared. It was all I could do to hold her and tell her that this wasn't going to hurt. He was just measuring her leg and needed to write on a few places. It wasn't until the car ride home that it hit me. The last time someone wrote on her leg, she took a very long nap and then woke up without a foot. Could she really remember that? I didn't know what to make of it, but I do know how scared she was by him writing on her leg. Mr. Karl also took a mold of her left foot and did some measurements there so that the next time we came back, he could have not only her new prosthesis, but also a shoe for her left foot. How exciting!

At the same time as all of this, I had discovered that we were expecting our third child. We had planned and hoped for another child, and a year earlier when it was time to try again, we were in the middle of chemotherapy with Sydnee. It just wasn't possible for us to try at that time. As crazy as it sounds, we thought our lives had slowed down some. Why not try for another child? We hadn't told anyone about this baby yet because it was so early in the pregnancy. I was trying to place my trust in God that this baby was going to be okay, but after having a child like Sydnee where her syndrome wasn't genetic and it just happened, I was a little worried and fearful. Deep down, I felt like something was wrong with the pregnancy because I wasn't feeling the early feelings I had felt with both of the girls. I put those worries out of my mind and dismissed the concerns as that I was now too busy to pay attention to all of the little early changes to my body.

My fears were founded when at eight weeks we went to my obstetrician for our first visit and ultrasound. I was quiet today because I knew something was wrong, but I was still hopeful that I was just being crazy. Upon ultrasound, they didn't see anything. They called it a blighted ovum. To me, it was a miscarriage and it was devastating.

How could this happen? Better yet, I knew all along something wasn't right. Why didn't I trust my gut? Why would God allow me to get pregnant only to lose the baby? My mind was full of questions that I certainly didn't have the answers to. Dr. Beckner said he really didn't want to put me through surgery to clean everything up because usually everything would pass in two weeks or so. He offered a pain prescription, but I wouldn't take it. I think I just needed to get out of the office and be alone.

Scott was there with me, but he had to go back to work. So, I did the only thing I knew how to do. I went home and picked up my girls from the sitter and then went shopping. I had received a phone call earlier as we were sitting in the doctors' office that Scott's sister thought she was going into labor today. We would have a new nephew perhaps that very afternoon. I needed to get something for my niece and nephew to make them feel special. The girls and I went to the card store looking for the perfect welcome baby cards and big brother/big sister cards. Talk about tough to do. We still hadn't told anyone yet that we were expecting. I was walking alone with the dark cloud over my head feeling that I had felt with Sydnee's pregnancy. I felt like I had a secret that I was keeping from our kids and from everyone else. It wasn't that we didn't want to tell people, it was just that I always tried to wait until after we saw the heartbeat to tell our families and then friends. Now, we had to tell everyone that not only were we pregnant, but we also had miscarried. I knew they wouldn't know what to say and that it would only make them feel bad for us. For now, the easier thing to do was to keep quiet. I knew we were going home to West Virginia in a few weeks, and we could share the news then. Along with that, how could we crush the possible exciting news of another nephew coming and steal their joy by telling them of our pain. We thought it best to wait until after this little guy arrived to tell our news, especially if he was coming so soon.

Our nephew was finally born about a week later and the baby still hadn't passed from inside of me. We were able to meet our newest nephew the day he was born. I was very nervous going to the hospital and not sure how I would react, but I knew I needed to go. I wanted to. I remember meeting him for the first time and holding him. It was so strange to be holding a beautiful miracle from God while at the same time knowing the baby inside of me had died. Part of me wanted to hold the new baby forever and never give him up while the other part of me needed to get out of that room and fast. It just so happened that our girls along with their other cousins were getting tired because it was in the late evening by now and we needed to get them home for bed. I was thankful for my beautiful little girls and full of questions at the same time.

It took about two weeks for the baby to pass and I was thankful Scott was home with me when it did. I made it through everything okay and still don't know if I have any more answers today as to why my baby didn't make it, but I do know that I have a special little someone waiting to meet me one day when I get to Heaven. Talk about something to look forward to! I don't even know if it is a boy or girl! It definitely is a great reminder of how fragile life here is. I didn't need another reminder of this, but I am even more aware of this every day.

By the middle of November we were finally able to take Sydnee back to Mr. Karl to get her prosthesis and shoe. She was a little skeptical at first, but once she saw him, she knew where we were and that she wasn't going to get poked. We tried on her prosthesis first and it fit perfectly! Her left shoe was next, and boy was she excited! We stood her up on the floor. She smiled at first and then was a little hesitant. It lasted only briefly before she started taking steps ever so slowly and wobbly, but she was walking nonetheless! She was able to have a shoe on her left foot for the first time. I snapped pictures as quickly as I could. Big sister Kerri was thrilled for Sydnee and held her hand as she walked down the hallway. God had brought us to this point finally but faithfully, and He was with us every step of the way.

Come Sunday morning, we were all so excited to show our friends at church Sydnee's new shoes! Sydnee, was perhaps the most excited, but shy too.

Journal entry Sunday, Nov. 16, 2008

Today we let you both walk in to church by yourselves with your new prosthesis, Sydnee. You were so excited and a little shaky to show off walking in your new prosthesis. Kerri, you were ready and willing to walk with Syd.

Holding her hand for every step of the way. When we put you down to walk, Syd, you took off holding onto Kerri's hand. The look on your face when your "church shoes" (black patent leather) hit the tile floor was unforgettable! You grinned from ear to ear at the sound your new shoes made against the tile floor. How simple but large to me! You taught me not to forget about the little things in life. Don't ever take those moments for granted! I love you both with my whole heart! By the way, everyone at church loved watching you walk and move around. I love you!

Being little girls, both Kerri and Sydnee loved to play dress up. Most of my day was spent helping them change clothes and then hanging up the outfits they had just taken off. One of the crazy little things that came up because of Sydnee's feet was princess shoes. Kerri was able to wear any shoe that she wanted. Because of this, Sydnee would ask me frequently when she was going to get to wear princess shoes like Kerri. It broke my heart each time. We tried to let her wear one shoe on the prosthetic foot, but it made that leg too long and she would limp. Eventually, she would fall, and it just wouldn't work. I knew I had to do something. My friend Cindy helped me make princess clips out of hair bows and scrapbook supplies that we would clip onto her shoes that she had to wear. When we first put them on her shoes, she looked down at her feet and said, "Mommy, I'm a princess!" It was the sweetest thing! I was a proud mommy that day.

It wasn't always the big things, but the everyday little things that made me be creative and find ways to help my little girl fit in and be herself. Some things were easier to figure out, while other things made me work a little harder. I loved this part of my "job." Whenever we would get ready to go somewhere, I would have to plan out and think ahead to what we would be doing. Because Sydnee was so little and it required a lot of work for her to walk, we used a stroller a lot. If we were going somewhere that required a lot of walking, I would need to bring the most appropriate stroller for that need. Whenever we flew commercially, we just got used to taking the prosthesis off and passing it through the scanner by itself. The security always pointed out to us that we didn't have to do this, but it was easier to carry her through the tunnel scanner than to let her walk alone and then have to be pulled aside at two years old and be scanned by a wand all alone. This would scare her something silly because she had to stand behind the wall by herself with a stranger, and we couldn't be there with her.

Just when Sydnee was getting pretty good at walking with her prosthesis, we were headed back to Boston for another surgery on her left foot this time. It was February 2009, and we were there for the wedge resection of her left foot. In this surgery, they would remove two toes and a pizza slice-shaped portion of the foot in an effort to reduce the width of the foot so that she could fit into a normal shoe. Again, they told us to plan on being there for two weeks and that we would have many pre-op appointments the days before surgery. Whenever a kid with vascular anomalies is planning on having surgery, it is always a big deal and a lot of people need to take a look at her to make sure she is okay for surgery. The surgery lasted about three and a half hours, and when Dr. Kasser came out, he said, "Surgery could not have went better." What an answer to many prayers for us! Because it was an elective surgery, it still made me wonder and worry about her outcome. Her surgery was on a Thursday and she was discharged from the hospital to the hotel on Saturday. It always amazes me how quickly they can have surgery, a big one no less, and then be able to leave the hospital so soon. Don't get me wrong, it was always nice to be able to all be together in the hotel room instead of having our family separated in a hotel and hospital. While we were there, we always had the best of care, especially from our favorite nurses. Each time we had a follow up with Dr. Kasser, he would say the surgery went better than he had expected. I just knew that was the Lord's hand in all of it. He kept her safe and healthy and free from complications.

Sydnee stayed in a cast for a few months and then was able to get her new "shoe" by early May. It was pink and white on the inside, and she loved it! She smiled and picked it up and hugged it! By the end of May, we were back in Knoxville for another surgery to remove the screw from Sydnee's foot and to then be put back into a cast for a month. The only part of being back in the hospital that Sydnee liked was getting a hospital ID bracelet. How funny that the little things in life can be so big to her.

We had planned a beach vacation with Scott's family for this week and had to skip it due to this minor surgery and then cast. We didn't think it would be fair to take Sydnee to the beach with all of the sand and hot sun and have to be in a cast. Scott still had the time off for vacation, so we decided to take the girls to Chattanooga, Tennessee to see the trains, aquarium and the children's museum. While we were there, Kerri had an accident and fell through a small railing in the model train museum. She had cut the back of her head open and we knew she probably needed stitches. So, off we go to the local children's hospital with one child in a cast and the other's head bleeding. What would they think about us?!

On the car ride there, Kerri who was four and a half years old at the time kept asking us questions about what they were going to do with her at the hospital. Poor thing, she was so worried. After all, every time her sister went to the hospital, she had surgery, a cast, and a "straw" in her arm (an IV). After both her daddy and I had told her several times, Sydnee piped up from the seat beside her and said, "Kerri, this is really no big deal." I guess compared to what she had been through, it really wasn't! While we were there at the hospital, the child care specialists were trying to perk Kerri up a little so she wouldn't be so scared. They offered her a popsicle, games, stickers, anything they had. To which Kerri answered no. She just wanted one of us to hold her. Sydnee, on the other hand, wanted everything they had to offer. It was so silly. I think Sydnee was trying to catch up on all of the fun things she always missed out on while she was the patient!

The summer was well under way, and Sydnee was healing very nicely after her last surgery. She had her new special shoe and was doing pretty well walking in it. This was the summer before Kerri started school and we wanted to make it special. We took the girls to Disney World in early July to celebrate both of their birthdays.

God was working in my baby girl's life and now I could more clearly see what she thought of herself. I had always prayed that she would have this kind of attitude about her body image to where nothing would stop her. I now saw firsthand the beginnings of this in her own little words at the mere age of three.

In August, Kerri started kindergarten, and she loved it! Sydnee was having fun at home with me, and we were able to have special mommy and Sydnee time together while Kerri was at school all day. By church camp time in early August, we decided to let Sydnee stay the whole week with my parents there to have something fun for her. While she was there, she loved going to children's church services to see the puppets and sing. She had made several friends that week. One little boy in particular was a little worried about Sydnee's leg. He didn't know what to think. He asked Sydnee about it and my mom said Sydnee looked right at him and said, "You can touch it. It won't hurt you." Wow! How amazing she is! Again, God was helping her to be bold and unashamed of the wonderful blessing He created her to be.

Chapter 10

EXCITING TIMES

Sydnee, all on her own, decided she wanted to take dance lessons like Kerri. I asked the teacher Mrs. Melita if it was alright for Sydnee to try it out this year. She so desperately wanted to do everything just like her big sister Kerri. I knew there would be so many things in dance that would be more difficult for her to do, but at least she wanted to try. As her parents, we wanted to let her try several things to see what would come naturally to her and that she would be able to do without telling her right off the bat that she couldn't do this or that. I spoke with the dance teachers and wanted to see where they stood on the issue. We didn't expect perfection; we just wanted to give her the chance to try to do something that she so desperately wanted to try. Mrs. Melita agreed and was just about as excited as I was to see what Sydnee could do. So on the first day of class, Sydnee sat outside the dance studio waiting for them to open the door, and she looked a little nervous and excited at the same time. When they opened the door, Sydnee didn't want to go inside without Kerri. She found Mrs. Melita and asked, "Mrs. Lita, can Kerri go inside with me today?" And just like that, they both went inside the classroom and had a wonderful time. It didn't take many times like this for Sydnee to feel secure enough to go on her own. I love the bravery and self-sufficiency that she possessed. She wasn't afraid to ask for anything that she thought she needed.

It was around this time that we learned we were going to have another baby. I was so excited but a little nervous at the same time. We knew we definitely needed to see the heartbeat first before we could rest a little easier. Since we had miscarried the previous pregnancy, I was growing more anxious to get to the first doctor appointment and ultrasound. I was out shopping one evening and ran into the ultrasound technician, and she congratulated me on the pregnancy. She told me she saw on the schedule where I was to come in for my first appointment the next week. I was totally aware of how many days were left until I was able to come in because each day had become a countdown. I told her how anxious I was growing each day, and she offered to call me the next day to see if she could work me into her schedule for a quick ultrasound. I was overwhelmed and excited at the same time. The phone rang the next morning, and she had an opening for me to come in to get a quick peek at my growing baby. Talk about a blessing! The Lord provided so much peace by allowing me to have an early appointment. I was able to once again rest assured in the promise that the Lord would provide.

It may not seem like much, but for me and considering all that we have been through at this point, this little peek was exactly what I needed to calm my fears.

We waited a few more weeks to have the official first appointment with my doctor. Everything was progressing very well with the pregnancy. We finally felt safe enough to let our parents know about the upcoming grandbaby. We sent flowers to both of them with a note that was from "Baby Coen." They both were so surprised and excited at the same time. Our baby was scheduled to arrive the first week of April. We decided to tell the girls one evening at the dinner table. They were excited. Kerri more than Sydnee because I don't think Sydnee quite understood at this point. Kerri smiled from ear to ear and clapped her hands in excitement. She added that now we were going to be a "five family." I think she meant a family of five, but "five family" sounded so much cuter that we left it alone. For the remainder of the pregnancy, she told everyone we were becoming a "five family." Sydnee was excited because Kerri was excited. My sweet girls would now both be big sisters!

The time was going by so fast, and we were planning yet another surgery trip to Boston. It was going to be a quick trip there to fix the ASD with a device closure for Sydnee. She had already had one device placed to fix the hole, but it didn't seal it off completely. We had been watching it for a while now, and because we knew we would have more surgeries to face in the future, the surgeons felt like it was a good time to try another device. Kerri was now in school, so we decided not to take her on this trip. I think she was a little sad, but she had a field trip planned while we were gone. I guess that made it all better. It was the first time I had been that far away from Kerri. I was a little worried about it, but knew it made the most sense. It is such a struggle to balance being with one child while the other one was somewhere entirely different. My mom was able to come down to our house to take care of Kerri while we were gone, which meant the world to me.

It was now the beginning of October 2009 and we had made it safely to Boston. Our pre-op day went well, but long as usual. We met with every doctor we had met before including, cardiology, orthopedics, vascular anomaly clinic, lab, and X-rays. Everyone was amazed at how well Sydnee was doing. She was a little skeptical as to what we were doing there. We had told her that we needed to have her heart fixed again and that was all. She shouldn't need a cast, and she should be able to walk again pretty soon with her prosthesis. That was cool with Sydnee. As long as you told her what was going to happen to her, she was fine. She might not like it, but she needed to know ahead of time what was coming. It was the strangest thing. Of course, she would cry and get a little upset whenever she had blood work drawn or X-rays taken, but as long as we held her and talked to her the whole time, she didn't fight us or get too worked up. The Lord definitely had His hand on her.

I think He helped her to understand perhaps more than we thought. We tried to use words that she would understand and that wouldn't scare her, and in some strange way, she seemed to be content with it all. It could only be the hand of God upon her life. I am convinced.

Dr. Kasser, the orthopedist, was able to meet with us as well. He said he felt like Sydnee's left foot had continued to grow and was getting pretty large. His goal of fitting her into a more normal shoe was slipping away. We had told him how we tried to fit one of the widest tennis shoes that are made and it was still too tight on her foot. He was heartbroken to admit that there wasn't much else we could do to shrink the size of her foot to fit into a normal shoe so that she could wear matching shoes. It may not seem like a big deal, but to a little girl who loved shoes, it was. I knew that as she got older and came to realize more and more how she was different, she would want to have matching shoes. Dr. Kasser also said that by having to wear a special shoe on her left foot, it would hinder her from playing sports. Unfortunately, Dr. Kasser said we may want to consider amputating the left foot also so that when she got older, she wouldn't be as limited as she was now. She would be able to wear any shoe that she wanted and would have an easier time playing sports and being more active in general. Currently the shoe that she had was a foam type open shoe with a rubber bottom. It was attached to her foot by two Velcro straps that crossed over the top of her foot. It didn't provide any warmth or protection to her foot and toes. The goal of these surgeries was long-term. We wanted to think ahead to when she was older to what would give her the best life possible. It was strange to me how hearing him say the word "amputate" this time wasn't as big a punch in the gut as it was the first time. I hated the fact that we had put her through a foot surgery already to not gain much use or function to her, but it did show us that perhaps amputation was the best option. Maybe seeing what wasn't working helped me to accept what could work easier.

On the day of surgery Sydnee was quick to realize it was a big day for her. She whimpered as Poppy, my Dad, prayed for her before they took her to surgery. It was always so difficult to hand her over to the nurse. Many times, because she was so tiny, they carried her back to the OR in their arms. It made it seem a little less scary perhaps to her. Being carried instead of having to lay down on the hospital bed. She would cry and say she wanted Mommy. It broke my heart every time, and I struggled to hold it together and not cry in front of her. It is terribly difficult to force a smile to your face when everything in you wants to burst into tears and hold onto her.

The surgery went well, and they were able to successfully place a second device in her heart to seal the hole. The ASD was fixed. Check that one off of the list. Now we can move on to another item. When Sydnee woke up from the surgery, she was upset to learn she wasn't wearing her panties. She could care less that she had an accident in them after surgery, she just needed them on. Silly mommy that I am, I only took a few pairs of panties with us because they told me she would have to wear a dressing on her groin (where the cath was inserted for surgery) for a few days post op. I had packed pull ups so that it wouldn't be as tight on her leg as underwear was. She was a big girl now and didn't need to wear pull ups. So, being the independent little girl that she was, she decided if she couldn't wear panties, she wasn't going to wear anything at all. So there my little girl was, naked even without a hospital gown on, and covered with only a sheet. By the afternoon, she had slept a little more and was happier. She told everyone who would listen, "They fixed my heart!" She was so happy and talkative. We had accomplished our mission for being here.

She wanted to wear her clip-on earrings while she spent the night in the recovery room. Just another reminder that the small things in life are sometimes very important. It didn't take much to make her happy, just a pair of underwear and her clip-on earrings.

We made it back in Tennessee and were ready to see Kerri and for her to see us. The girls hugged and giggled with each other and were ready to play. It was so sweet to watch them interact with each other. I love that they were such good buddies. I know they will always be so close. Kerri has always been a great helper and supporter of Sydnee.

About two weeks later, we had to go see our cardiologist, Dr. Madhok, for Sydnee's post-op follow-up. Sydnee was a little skeptical about what we were going to do there. As soon as she realized she wasn't going to have to wear the white mask, she was fine. She remembered everything up until the point of sedation and was referring to the anesthesia mask she had to wear before going to sleep. Dr. Madhok said both of the cardiac devices were still in place and had not moved any since the surgery. Along with this, the right side of her heart was shrinking some and was almost back to a normal size. Praise the Lord! It is always great to hear that something was going right for Sydnee. The doctor also cleared Sydnee to go back to dance class. She was the most excited about that!

Later on that same day, we picked up Kerri from school and headed straight to the dance studio. Sydnee walked inside wearing a huge grin. She told her little friends that they fixed her heart. It was a great day to celebrate. At one point in the dance class, I looked in the window to check on Sydnee to see a few little girls fighting over who was going to stand beside her. That little three-year-old dance class was such a big support for Sydnee. They all were so sweet and loved to hear that Sydnee was doing well. It made my heart so happy to see Sydnee be so accepted doing something that she absolutely loved. You go, Sydnee!

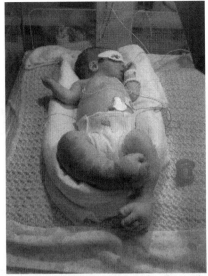

Sydnee in the NICU receiving phototherapy.

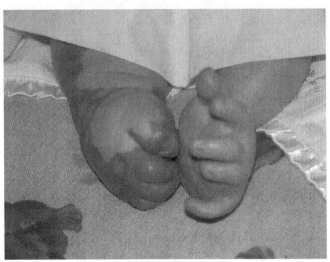

Her feet.

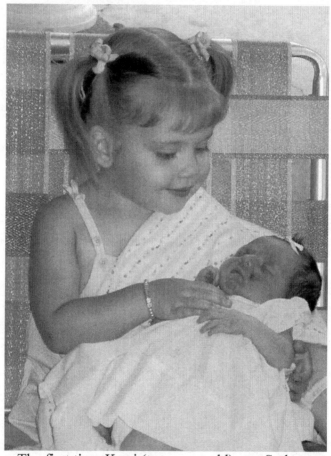

The first time Kerri (two years old) met Sydnee.

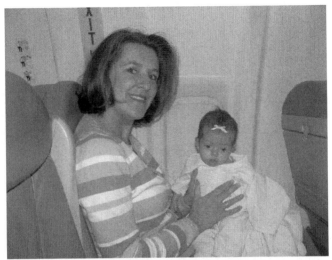

First trip to Boston.

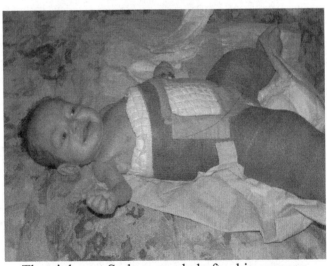

The pink cast Sydnee needed after hip surgery.

With big sister Kerri.

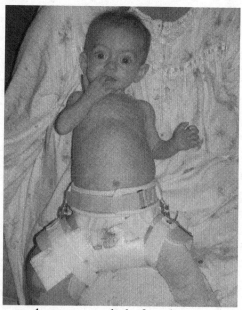

The brace that was needed after the cast came off.

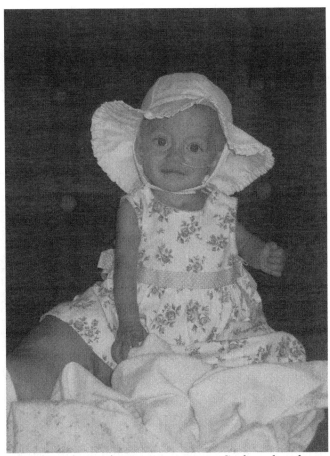

During chemotherapy treatments Sydnee lost her hair and had the NG tube.

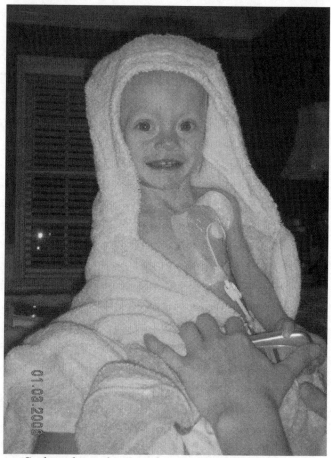

Sydnee kept the Broviac line in 24/7 while on chemo.

Finding any means to walk.

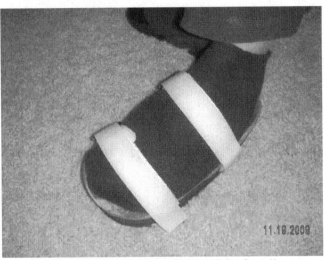

The Velcro shoe to fit her "big foot."

The day in the snow.

Sydnee's dance picture.

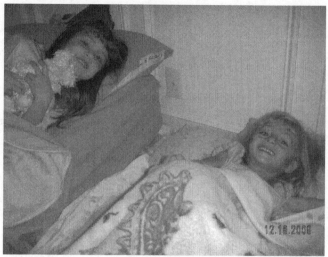

Kerri and Sydnee in their side-by-side twin beds.

Sydnee, Kerri and Noah when he was born. Sydnee had her blanket rubbing her lips.

The day all three kids were playing school.

My husband Scott and our three precious children.

Sydnee's marker with her handwritten name below.

It changed us all when we lost Sydnee. There will always be an empty space in our family without her. We choose to fill that space with love for God, Sydnee and each other.

Chapter 11

A GLIMPSE INTO SYDNEE'S LIFE

Very early on Sydnee began to notice she was a little different. She recognized before the age of two that she didn't have shoes. Being a shoe-lover myself, I remember worrying about how to downplay shoes while I was pregnant with her. I didn't know how I could explain to her about her feet. I began to do three-dimensional molds of her feet at various stages. I just feared that one day, she would be so angry at us for amputating her feet. It was my safety net. I would be able to show her firsthand what her feet looked like. I would make a mold before we had another surgery and at various stages in her first years of life. These molds were awesome. They captured every wrinkle even down to the toenails.

One day while we were getting dressed to run some errands, I was telling Kerri to get her shoes on so we could go. Sydnee looked at me and said, "Mommy, I no have shoes; I have socks." She knew the difference between her and Kerri at that point.

I answered, "Yes, I know, Sydnee, but we pray that one day, you will have shoes to wear on your feet just like Kerri." It broke my heart, but I was determined to make the best of it for her. This was the way that God created her to be, and He knew better than we did. It just meant we needed to be a little creative. This was about the time when girls' socks came out decorated like shoes. We had some in every color.

In the summer of 2009 when Sydnee had just turned three years old, we were on vacation at the beach. Kerri had already made a little friend while we were at the pool one afternoon. The next day, Sydnee was playing in the baby pool where she was the most comfortable. Because she didn't wear her prosthetic while in the water, she could reach the bottom of the pool a little easier in the baby pool. Along with this, she didn't have much body fat and got cold really quickly in the bigger pools even in the middle of the day in the hot sun. It didn't matter the weather, she would only last about fifteen minutes or so in the big pool before her teeth would begin to chatter and her little lips would start to turn a purplish blue color.

She loved to "cook" in the baby pool or on the side of the pool using bowls, spoons, whatever she could find to play with. On this particular day, Kerri and her new friend came over to the baby pool to play with Sydnee. I told Kerri she should introduce her friend to her sister. Kerri, being the shy one, didn't want to, but Sydnee caught right on and introduced herself to the little girl. I sat there beside the girls and listened as Sydnee said her name and then noticed the little girl looking at her left foot. She immediately explained, "I had surgery, and they took a screw out of my foot, and that's why it looks like that." She didn't say anything about her right foot missing, but I was still shocked at how matter-of-fact Sydnee had handled herself. She knew clearly that she was different and that others were aware, but it didn't seem to bother her.

When Sydnee was about three and a half years old, we took the girls to the ice skating rink for the first time. Kerri was so very excited. She had wanted to ice skate for some time. We had been told that the ice rink would have a sled of some type that we could pull Sydnee around the ice in as a form of modified ice skating for her. Once we got there, we asked them about the sled and they acted like they had no idea what we were talking about. They didn't have anything like that at all. I felt like such a bad mommy for not calling ahead and checking it out. Poor Sydnee—she was so disappointed. We had built it up to be so much fun and now she wasn't going to be able to participate. I was pregnant and not able to get on the ice, so that just left Scott. He took Kerri around the rink a few times while Sydnee helped me take pictures. Scott hadn't been ice skating in many years, so he wasn't very sure of his ability to carry her around the rink, so we had to think of an alternative very quickly. Scott decided to try to walk around the rink with Sydnee while holding onto the rail. She was so excited and grinned from ear to ear. She kept talking about how slippery and cold the ice was. It was really cool to watch Sydnee be able to try something new.

Christmas was approaching in 2009, and we were all getting more excited. It just so happened that on Kerri's last day of school before Christmas break we were getting snow! Growing up as kids in West Virginia, Scott and I both were very used to getting snow and occasionally having a snow day from school. Our kids, however, hadn't really ever experienced much snow living in Tennessee. When we would get snow, it seemed like it was always two inches or less which isn't really that much fun to play in. This time we received about seven inches of snow! I don't know who was more excited, the girls or us! Scott went out to buy snow shovels and sleds because we didn't have any. We dressed the girls as warm as we could and took them outside to build a snowman. We had a blast together playing out in the cold snow. Little Sydnee didn't like walking around in the deep snow very much. I think because she was so short and the snow was so deep; it was pretty difficult for her to move around much in it. Her prosthesis was harder to move around because it needed to be lifted up out of the snow to take another step instead of dragging her leg through the snow. Along with this, her foot was getting wet from the snow. Sydnee did have a shoe for her left foot, but it was open with Velcro straps holding it across her foot. We tried to put as many pairs of panty hose and socks on her as we could in an attempt to keep her leg and foot as warm and dry as possible.

We finished building the snowman as a family and then moved on to making snow angels and throwing snowballs. By this time, Sydnee was cold and crying. She was ready to go inside and get warmed up. When I checked my watch, I realized we had been outside for about an hour and a half. We came in and started undressing the girls to get off their wet clothes. It was only then that we realized exactly how wet Sydnee's foot had gotten and how cold she was. Her poor little socks were dripping wet! We felt so bad. She was probably hurting from being so cold and wet. We took the girls straight to the bathtub to get warmed up and dry. It was another reminder that maybe amputating her left foot would help with allowing her to be more free to play outside on days like this. We tried as best we could to keep her foot dry and warm, but an open shoe just wasn't going to work in cold weather. It was things like this that made it so much easier for us to make the decision of amputation. It was a wonderful day outside to play in the freshly fallen snow. Definitely one I won't forget.

On Christmas Eve, the girls helped us set out hot chocolate and cookies for Santa, and we put them to bed. When the girls woke up on Christmas morning, Kerri was ready to open presents, but all that Sydnee cared about was getting her Pop Tart and orange juice. Once she had that, she was ready to take on the day. My little Sydnee loved to eat especially breakfast, and she always wanted a chocolate Pop Tart with the sides and top torn off and the bottom left alone. She was particular in what she wanted, and she felt she needed to remind us of this order every morning.

Chapter 12

BOSTON AGAIN

It was January 2010, and we were headed to Boston once again for a very big surgery for Sydnee. It was the time when the swine flu was big, so the hospital wouldn't let anyone under the age of eighteen in the hospital besides those who were patients. Because of this, we couldn't take Kerri with us on this trip because she wouldn't be allowed in the hospital. Along with this, she was also now in school, and we knew missing two weeks of school was going to be a big deal. We made arrangements for Kerri and planned our trip. I was 27 weeks pregnant now with our third child and growing very anxious about the upcoming surgery for Sydnee, being away from Kerri for this long, and worried about me getting up there and back safely without going into preterm labor. It was a lot to handle and process, but I was trusting God for His timing and His purpose in all of this.

The morning we were packing up our car to go to the airport, we saw four bluebirds on the driveway sitting so still and looking carefree. Our friend Shep had called to pray with us before we left. We told him about seeing the bluebirds, and he reminded us of the scripture passage where it talks about the sparrows of the field and that if God cared enough for them, then surely He cared for us and was close to us today.

Along with this, our morning devotion was this: "Never look ahead to the changes and challenges of this life in fear. Instead, as they arise, look at them with the full assurance that God, whose you are, will deliver you out of them. Hasn't He kept you safe up to now? So hold His loving hand tightly, and He will lead you safely through all things. And when you cannot stand, He will carry you in His arms.

"Do not look ahead to what may happen tomorrow. The same everlasting Father who cares for you today will take care of you tomorrow and every day. Either He will shield you from suffering, or He will give you unwavering strength that you may bear it. Be at peace then, and set aside all anxious thoughts and worries" (Frances de Sales, *Streams in the Desert*).

The day came for us to leave, and Kerri and Sydnee were so pitiful. They sat in the van on the way to the airport holding hands. It just about broke my heart listening to them saying their goodbyes. They were best buddies, and I knew this trip would also be tough on Kerri being left out and alone while the rest of her family went away. I can't imagine going through all of this at five and a half years old. We tried to keep the "see-yas" brief so that no one would burst into tears, myself included, and we were able to board the airplane and be on our way. On the first flight, Sydnee looked at Scott and then me and said, "This is my special day with both of you." Talk about pulling on your heart; she didn't realize all that was coming her way. On the second flight, she had fallen asleep on my lap and the stewardess made me wake her up about twenty minutes before we were to land. She cried most of the rest of the flight because I think she now knew what was going on. She had lots of questions the rest of the evening and wanted to know in detail what was going to happen.

We were able to settle Sydnee down and get her to sleep in the hotel that night. We all had lots on our minds and knew we would need to be clear-minded for all of the pre-op appointments we had scheduled. During the early-morning hours, we were awakened with a text message sent to Scott's cell phone. We looked at the hotel alarm clock and saw it was 3:00 am and wondered who would be texting us at this time. It scared us to death, but when he checked it, he saw a message from his friend that lived out west in a different time zone. In his message, he said he wasn't able to sleep and had an urgency that he needed to text us right now to let us know he was praying for Sydnee and for us. As we were trying to lie back down to go back to sleep, we looked at the message on the phone again and noticed the time on Scott's phone said 6:00 am, but the alarm clock in the room was three hours slow. Had this friend not paid attention to God's leading, we might have overslept because of the silly alarm clock. Already, we knew God was in control and that he was right there with us guiding us every step of the way.

We had appointments starting at 8:00 am the next day with Interventional Radiology and Cardiology. We were at the hospital most of the day and worn out by the evening. Sydnee was scheduled to have a Venogram (an X-ray that takes pictures of the blood flow through the veins in a certain area of the body) and possible IVC (Inferior Vena Cava) filter placement. She was getting more and more nervous because the procedure was delayed by something else in the hospital. We assured her that this was not surgery; she was just going to have some pictures taken while she was sleeping and that seemed to relieve her fears somewhat. You have to remember, she was barely three and a half years old by now, but we tried to tell her as much as she could handle with terms that she was able to understand. It was a long morning and day.

She came through the procedure pretty well, and they did wind up placing an IVC filter. I knew they were just being as careful as possible, but now she would need to have another procedure to remove it a few days after surgery on her leg. She and I had to spend the night in the hospital that night as a precaution. She was okay with it because I was staying in her room with her and because her favorite nurse was taking care of her again.

The morning of the big surgery, the floor nurse said she would take my personal items to the ICU for us, but I told them they only booked an ICU bed for her because of the surgery like they always had before. It was just a protocol they had to follow and that Sydnee should be back on this floor later today. The nurse looked at me like I was silly, but I didn't think much of it. They came for Sydnee around 6:30 am, and it was an emotional time for all of us. She was so quiet and definitely worried. When we loaded up in the elevator, I saw the tears begin to roll down her cheeks so softly. She wasn't crying out loud, but she was definitely afraid. She held onto my hand so tightly. My heart was breaking into so many pieces. I wanted to do nothing else but to scoop her up off of the bed and run down the hallway with her. It was so hard to handle the fact that we had chosen this for her.

Once we were in the holding area, the doctors started to show up and squeeze in a quick pre-op appointment for us to discuss the surgery and to sign the consent. She looked at me while the doctors were talking and asked me, "Why do I have to have surgery?" I honestly didn't have a chance to answer her question because just as quick as they asked, they gave her the "sleepy medicine" (Versed). The doctors were still talking to us and marking her legs before I realized she had gone to sleep.

Her question was still lingering in the air, and I wasn't able to answer it before she went to sleep. They came to take her back to surgery and Scott was allowed to walk back with her and wait until she was in the OR. It was the time to give her kisses and to whisper a thousand "I love yous" and "I'll see you when you wake up." I was fighting back the tears because I didn't want her to see me get so upset. I was her mommy and I needed to be strong for her.

They couldn't tell us exactly how long the surgeries would take, but that it would be a while. They called on our cell phones to say they had started with the first incision at 8:30 am. Dr. Kasser, the orthopedist, began work on amputating her left foot and came out to talk with us around 10:45 am. He told us she was doing fine and that he thought we made the right choice to amputate her foot. Later, the other doctor would tell us that Dr. Kasser was very sad to have to amputate her foot. He said he heard Dr. Kasser say, "We were so close to getting where we needed to be." He wished so badly that we could have saved her foot.

It was so reassuring to us that someone else thought we made the right choice. I needed to hear that. They began work on her right leg around 11:00 am. Here they were re-amputating one of the bones in her right leg because it had continued to grow and was starting to bruise the bottom of her stump. They said this was to be expected in this type of amputation in someone her age because she was still growing.

Along with this, they were also removing a section the length of her leg in an effort to reduce the circumference of her right leg. This was the longest portion of the surgery because they would have to move so slowly because of all of the extra vascularization in her leg due to her syndrome. This part of the day seemed to drag on so slowly. As the day progressed, I was beginning to physically ache because I needed to see my baby girl. This was by far her longest and biggest surgery ever, and I was worried.

Finally, by 6:25 pm the nurse called and said they were closing up and that Dr. Fishman, the vascular surgeon, would be out to talk with us soon. It had been a ten hour surgery, but as of now, she was fine. When he finally came out to talk with us, he said everything went well, but that she had lost a lot of blood, and they had transfused her with a lot. He said she was going to need to spend at least one night in the ICU which was a complete shock to us. I just knew that meant she was bad and was all the more desperate to see her. The doctor felt bad that we didn't know about the ICU, but I guess he had planned on her going there all along. Now thinking back, that floor nurse must have thought I was crazy or something. Her funny look now made sense to me. We were completely in the dark on this one, but still trusting. The doctor also said that she had been and was still in good hands because his favorite anesthesiologist was working with her today. He hadn't requested him to work on Sydnee's case, but that it just worked out that way. God was still in charge.

We were finally able to scoot up to the ICU to find Sydnee extubated (off of the ventilator) and breathing on her own. She was still groggy and sleepy, but opened her eyes as best as she could to see us. Her little face was so swollen and puffy, but she was okay. I was able to kiss her and hold her hand, and it felt so good. God had been so close to her and kept her safe in His hands. My heart was still heavy with worry but also filling with thankfulness and praise. I was able to spend the night with her in her ICU room and help out with her during the night.

By Friday, they thought she was doing well enough to go to a regular room. We were back on the same floor as we had spent so many nights post-op before and back to familiar faces. She was more comfortable and able to rest here. It wasn't until then that we discovered exactly how much blood Sydnee had lost during her surgery. They told us she had lost an adult's total blood volume which was replaced of course, but she had never needed blood with a surgery before. This was definitely bigger than we had realized going into it.

By Saturday, we took her off of the morphine pump and placed her on oral medications. That evening, the itching started. By Sunday, it was post-op day three and the itching was worse and she was so whiny. All of the grandparents were going home, and I think that made her a little more emotional as well. It would now just be her, Scott and me up there to recover the rest of the time. Her favorite nurse was back on shift this evening and she came bearing gifts of barbecue chips, carrots, and ranch dressing. Sydnee's favorites!

The next day continued with more and more itching. There wasn't much we could do because her legs were covered in dressings and we weren't allowed to change them until Tuesday, five days post-op. The nurses had reassured us that this itching was normal for most of their patients and the one thing that bothered them the most post-op. It was amazing to me that this little thing was becoming such a big deal when she had had a much bigger surgery this time. She didn't complain of pain, it was the itching that was the problem. The morning of the dressing change, Sydnee was a little quiet and worried. She held her blanket so tightly to her lips (a common thing for Sydnee and her one comfort item). The doctors said the incisions looked great, and Dr. Fishman went as far to say that we could go home to Tennessee that same day. We were shocked! Then, he remembered that she still had the IVC filter in place, so because of that, we would have to get the opinion of the interventional radiologist before the final decision was made.

When we finally heard back from them, they didn't feel comfortable taking the filter out so quickly, so this meant we would have to stay in Boston for two more weeks. We were able to be discharged from the hospital to the hotel, however, and it was a little easier to relax and let the three of us be a family together in the same room instead of being split up with Scott at the hotel and Sydnee and me at the hospital.

By Monday of the next week, we went back to the hospital for Sydnee's IVC filter removal and more post-op visits with both of the surgeons. It was a good day to be able to get rid of the filter and possibly get the final word on us being able to go home. Sydnee was a little nervous, but she was being so brave. She tolerated the procedure very well, and they gave us the filter to keep as a souvenir. When we went to see both Dr. Kasser and Dr. Fishman, they both commented on how well Sydnee was doing so soon after surgery. Dr. Fishman was amazed at how well Sydnee could move her right leg. He did notice some blackened areas forming along the incision line. He knew this was possible. He said it would get worse before it got better, though. He talked us through how to do the dressing changes as well as continuing to manage the drains that were still in her leg. We would have to continue to empty them twice a day and record the drainage amounts to report to them once a week. When the drainage slowed down, we would then have to remove them somewhere in Kingsport. Sydnee was so excited to hear the news that we were allowed to go home. She was missing being home and missing her big sister Kerri as we all were.

Tuesday couldn't come fast enough for any of us. We made it home safely and practically ran in the airport to get to Kerri as soon as possible. Kerri looked so big and grown up standing there at the end of the terminal doors. She was smiling from ear to ear, and after a big hug to Sydnee, she was able to jump into my arms. It had been a long time to be away from my Kerri. I don't ever want to be away from her that long again. I had missed her something awful.

While at home, we had to adapt to a new routine of Lovenox injections and dressing changes twice a day. The dressing changes were more involved this time around and were most definitely a two-person job. We had to start waking up Sydnee a few minutes earlier each day so that we could get the dressing change completed while Scott was still at home before going to work. She was able to help out with her own dressing change now. She loved being a part of it and eagerly asked to help out by holding the dressing in place or rerolling the ace wraps so that they would be ready when we needed them.

I was growing more and more pregnant by this time with about six weeks left to go before my due date. Sydnee's legs had not healed to the point where we could get her fitted for her prosthesis, so whenever we went anywhere, we had to take a stroller for her to ride in. For the most part, she didn't mind it, but whenever we were around other kids who could run and play independently, I could tell she was a little sad about not having her legs to move. After about four weeks, she was able to go back to physical therapy with Mrs. Jill, and she was so excited. Playing all of the games there and doing "exercises" as Sydnee called them was a great day!

Sydnee's right leg did get a lot worse before it ever got better. At one point, the darkened areas on her leg had turned completely black and were tough like leather. The doctors told us it would come off like a scab and would then need to heal from the inside out. We were delicately caring for this now large wound the best way we knew how. We talked with a local surgeon who suggested we use silver nitrate sticks around the edges of her good skin to stimulate new skin growth. The only problem with this was that it stung. Poor little Sydnee—she was trying to be so brave, but she usually cried on the nights when we had to use the "stick" as she called it. We did everything to try to help it heal quicker and for it not to sting. I would hold a battery-powered fan over her leg while Scott would use the stick just to help cool it off a little.

By the middle of March, Sydnee was desperate to go back to see her friends at dance class. She would ask me every week if it was her turn again. Finally, I felt like it was safe to return back and talked with Mrs. Melita and Miss Devan to see if they minded her coming back even though she didn't have feet to stand on. Sydnee was able to crawl around on the floor and scoot wherever she wanted or needed to, and she was also still so small that we carried her around. The teachers were more than happy to allow her to come back and were so excited to see her again. The other little girls were excited to see Sydnee again that they all squealed and hugged her. It was a sweet moment for this mommy to observe. Sydnee was so excited and brave going into the class, but started to cry as I was leaving. To help ease her fears, I sat in the corner of the room and watched for a few minutes with Sydnee on my lap. After a few minutes, she was smiling and counting to eight and tapping her leg on the floor while the other girls were tapping their toes. Sydnee showed them you didn't have to have toes to tap the beat.

God was still working in her life, even though we couldn't always see it so easily. Normal day-to-day life was sometimes a little tricky to maneuver, but we managed and tried to have a positive attitude for Sydnee and Kerri. They were watching us and soaking up everything.

Chapter 13

A BABY MAKES A FIVE FAMILY

On Tuesday, March 30, 2010 we welcomed our third child and first son into the world. We named him Noah Scott Coen which means peaceful and provider of comfort. Life had been a little crazy and I knew God had blessed us with another most precious gift. He was a peanut of a baby and fit right in to our family perfectly. Yes, he was our third living child, but he just seemed to fit right in very smoothly. We had heard that having three children was busy and at times, I guess it was, but I just really remember life being so calm and beautiful.

We were still having chemotherapy follow-up appointments every three months as well as kidney ultrasounds, cardiology appointments, blood work, and well child visits for Noah and the girls. Life was busy, and I spent a lot of time on the road with the two younger kids while Kerri was in school. Sydnee's leg still hadn't healed completely, so we were still waiting around on that as well. By the end of April, we were finally able to see the prosthestist, Mr. Karl, to start getting measurements for Sydnee's new prostheses. It was an exciting day. He said it would take him a few weeks to work on it and then he would get back to us. We didn't care, just being able to get this far was exciting!

One day Sydnee came to me and wanted to know when she was going to have "skin legs" like Kerri. I was a little taken aback by her question but wanted to know truly what she was asking and why. We sat down on the steps and talked. At this point, Sydnee's leg was still healing, and we didn't have her new prostheses yet, so she wasn't able to walk by herself. She had been this way since her last surgery in January, so I was sure she was getting tired of having to be carried around or crawling around on the floor like a baby. I answered her as best I could and told her that we were doing all that we could do to help her big leg heal as quickly as possible. This answer seemed to suffice for the time being, but she continued to ask me several different times over a month period about getting her new "skin legs." At this point, I was beginning to think that she thought she was going to have perfect little legs like her big sister Kerri. Only then did it hit me that she was again noticing that she was different. It was a difficult conversation to have with a three-and-a-half-year-old but obviously one that was now necessary. We talked about how God made Sydnee special and one of the special things about her was her legs. She was going to get legs that she could take on and off instead of ones that stayed on all of the time. God makes everyone a little different, and sometimes it is easier to see our differences. She seemed satisfied with those answers but continued to want to talk about it in times when it was just Sydnee and me. I'm so thankful that she felt comfortable to talk with me about her feelings in the best way she could.

Sydnee was still attending weekly dance class, and recital time was quickly approaching. I met with the teachers and told them that Sydnee didn't have to be in the recital; just coming to class each week was enough. They didn't want to hear any part of it and insisted it wasn't a big deal to change the routine so that Sydnee could be included. It blessed my heart because down deep I was hoping she could have this opportunity, but didn't expect her to have it. I knew Sydnee would always need some modifications, I just didn't want people to think I expected them to change because of her.

The recital weekend came and both of the girls were so excited to show off their hard work. Kerri was tap dancing with her class this year and Sydnee was dressing up as a bunny for her routine. Each of the girls in Syd's group used a hot pink chair as a prop while Sydnee sat in hers. They were bunnies being pulled out of a big black hat by the magician who danced with Sydnee while she sat in her chair. Sydnee did what she could and exactly what she was told to do. She clapped her little hands and tapped her legs while seated in the chair as the other little girls danced around her and with her. I sat there and watched her shine with a bright smile on her face. Tears streamed down my face not in feeling sorry for her, but in immense pride and a sense of relief for her. Yes, we had made the difficult decision to amputate not one, but both of her feet. But, she still kept that precious smile on her face. It was as much a lesson for me as a lifestyle for her. No matter what we face, God is right there with us cheering us on, encouraging us not to give up. The true joy comes through the pain.

The week after the dance recital Mr. Karl, the prosthetist, called us to say Sydnee's prostheses were ready. We were planning a trip close to that area on the weekend, so we decided we could go on Saturday for this next fitting. Kerri was performing with our church kids at a talent competition that same day, so we decided Scott would take Sydnee for the fitting while I kept Kerri and Noah at the competition. We drove halfway Friday night and spent the night there, and our church van picked the kids and me up the next morning to ride the rest of the way with them while Scott and Sydnee remained behind to wait for the fitting.

A few hours later, Scott sent me a picture of Sydnee's new legs from his phone. It was so cool to see her upright again standing on two legs with two feet. Scott also said that the new prosthesis for the right leg wasn't the final one, but one that she could use now. It was made like her first one and attached to her leg with Velcro straps wrapped around her leg. It just wasn't going to be practical for her now that she was older and more active. We didn't mind, though; just having her be able to walk again would mean so much to her.

When they arrived at the place where we were, it was the best feeling ever to see the children get so excited for Sydnee. They clapped and cheered as she shyly walked towards us. Her legs were pretty wobbly, and she needed to hold on to her daddy's hands to help stabilize herself. I was able to video her walking again for the first time on two prostheses. Even through my tears, I still remember what an awesome moment it was to see her shy smile spread all over her face. We all gave her big hugs and she was able to show the other children her cute little toes. There weren't any shoe stores close by, so we did the next best thing: we went across the road to Walmart! She chose a hot pink jelly type shoe and wore them out of the store. She was so excited to show Kerri and the other kids.

Later, on our way home, we stopped at another shoe store and went a little crazy with shoe shopping. Scott didn't mind, he just smiled. He knew it was a big deal to be able to buy practically any pair of shoe that she wanted because we knew they would now fit her little feet. Always before we would only use the right shoe. Now we were interested in both shoes and lots of them! Along with this, her shoe size had changed to a nine which meant she wouldn't have any shoes at home that would fit her new little feet. Little Sydnee thought we were going to turn in the hot pink shoes from earlier and started to cry when we were trying on the other new shoes. I reassured her that we would keep those shoes, but that we would want a few other pairs to match other clothes. With that bit of reassuring news, she was smiling again and asking for several pairs of shoes with one stipulation: that they were "just like Kerri's."

The next day was Sunday, and that meant

there was another exciting place to go show off Sydnee's new legs...our church. We all got ready for church and took a few pictures of Sydnee standing on her new legs with her shiny new patent leather shoes. As we let her walk into the foyer at church, it was such a blessing to behold. Sydnee grinning from ear to ear and Kerri talking a mile a minute eager to show Sydnee off. I watched as several of our dear church family were moved to see her upright again and walking. They had been such big prayer warriors for Sydnee, and to see such a blessing unfolding right before their eyes was awesome.

The following Wednesday night, we were at church, and Sydnee needed to go potty. I don't know why, but both of my little girls loved to have big discussions while going potty. I took her, and while we were in the restroom together, she looked at me and said, "Mommy, I'm sure glad I'm back to normal." I acted as though I didn't hear what she said and asked her to repeat it as a stall tactic because I was caught off guard. She repeated herself. I asked her what she meant by that, and in true Sydnee fashion, she raised her hands in the air and rolled her eyes and said, "You know, my new legs."

To that, I said, "Oh, so having your legs is normal for you?"

She answered, "Yes." I was so glad that she was able to accept herself and that she considered having two prostheses as her "normal."

Summer was here, and Kerri was out of school. We knew that traveling with an infant wouldn't be much fun, so we tried to come up with several mini-vacations throughout the summer. Even though Noah was an excellent baby, we still didn't think it would be much fun to take him to the beach and have to worry about him getting sunburned. Scott was trying to take Mondays off, so we tried to use them as family days. We would go to the pool together or even to Dollywood. We surprised the girls with buying season passes there, and they were over the moon! They loved all of the kiddie rides.

Summertime also brought the girls' birthdays. Their birthdays are three days apart, so we have always had one party with two birthday cakes. Since Kerri was in school and had met new friends, we thought it might be nice for her to have her own party. Not having family living close, we decided to have two different parties but hold them at the same time. Sydnee invited some of her friends from dance class and Kerri invited some from school and dance class. We held the parties at our house but had them overlapping so that they wouldn't be in the same place at the same time. I spent most of the afternoon running back and forth, but my girls had a wonderful time and both felt special. That was enough for me.

With new birthdays always comes well child checkups. We scheduled both of the girls' checkups at the same time, but I made sure Scott was off of work and could go with me. Kerri went first because she was the most nervous. I knew she didn't need any vaccinations, but I wasn't sure about blood work or urine. When she was finished, she was relieved, but still worried about the finger poke. Scott took Kerri and went to the lab while I stayed back with Sydnee and Noah. Sydnee stood by the exam table and wrote her name on the exam paper for the first time! I was so excited! I knew she knew how to do it, she just hadn't ever wanted to write all of the letters in the correct order before. So, as a proud mommy, I tore off the part of the paper and kept it.

Sydnee needed some vaccines, and she tolerated them pretty well. We then scooted over to find Scott and Kerri in the lab. Kerri was crying because of her sore finger, and then Sydnee began to cry. I asked her why she was crying and she said that she wanted to get her finger poked. Go figure!

Sydnee had always been fascinated with fingernail polish and getting manicures and pedicures. I wasn't really sure how nail polish would stick to a prosthetic foot, so I hadn't polished her toenails yet. We were staying with my parents for a few days in the summer and I thought it would be a great thing for all of us girls to experience together. Kerri picked out her color and wanted to get a design on her toenails also. Not to be left out, Sydnee wanted a flower design just like Kerri's. Sydnee watched as the nail tech cleaned off all of the old polish on Kerri's toes and repolished them. Next was Sydnee's turn. She climbed up into the pedicure chair and watched very intently. She sat quietly for a while and then looked at me first and then at her Nana and asked, "Where's the water?" She knew that everybody soaked their feet first before polishing them, and she had skipped that part. I had to explain to her that we couldn't soak her feet today and she accepted that and moved on. With metal ankles, we knew it wasn't good to get them wet.

It was now time for the design. She chose pink nail polish with a white flower on her big toenails just like Kerri's. Mimi, my friend, came over and started to place the first flower on her toenail. She asked Sydnee what color she wanted the center of the flower to be. In true Sydnee fashion, she answered, "Pink." Mimi tried to explain to her that since the toenail was already painted pink, the center of the flower would not show up if it was the same color. After some discussion, Sydnee finally agreed to a purple center for the flower, but only on one toenail. The other flower center was going to be pink.

Mimi laughed and simply said, "I'll do it for you." She knew she wasn't going to win with this four-year-old.

As Mimi placed the purple dot on the first flower, she again asked Sydnee if she wanted both flowers to match, and Sydnee said no. As Mimi painted the second flower center pink, Sydnee very quietly said, "I told you I could see it." We all had to laugh at that one. She is definitely my independent one!

Summer was ending. Kerri had started back to school and was in the first grade. Sydnee and I were having lots of time together at home working on "school work" as she called it. We would do several pages of a preschool workbook each day in the mornings as her school. She was also getting lots of practice being a big sister and helping out with Noah. Church camp was also approaching back in West Virginia, and we weren't going to be able to go for the full time this year with Kerri already in school. Scott and I talked and decided Sydnee could go and stay with my parents while they were there, and we could pick her up on the weekend when we were able to go. She was so excited to be able to be the only one who could stay with Nana and Poppy and get to go to church camp without the rest of us. On Sunday afternoon, Scott decided he would fly Sydnee up there and stay for the evening service and then come home. I wanted to go, but figured Kerri didn't need to get home so late since she had school the next day.

While they were there, they decided to stay for the evening service, but Scott had only worn shorts and not taken pants with him. It wouldn't really matter, but I guess I have rubbed off on him that, in my opinion, he should always try to look his best especially for church. My mom actually talked him into staying, and he said it was a great service. My dad is a district superintendent in the Church of the Nazarene, so that meant for this week he would have to be on the platform helping out with the services. He told Scott that several people there had stopped him and asked him about how we were doing, especially Sydnee. Dad thought that it would be nice if the people could see her in her full glory, so to speak, at one time and on the platform. Scott was embarrassed to be wearing shorts and now he would have to take Sydnee on the platform during the service. Scott asked my mom to take her so he wouldn't have to be up there with shorts on. When it came time for her, my mom took her to the platform on the side and let her walk across it to my dad. Scott said it was so special to be able to sit back and watch her from a distance walking, grinning from ear to ear. Several people in the congregation were shouting praises to God and clapping. They were seeing firsthand and many of them for the first time this year God's faithfulness and hand at work in someone's life for whom they had so diligently prayed. She was a living miracle. Not in the sense that physically she was healed and never to suffer hardships or surgeries again, but that God's hand was evident in so many aspects of her life. We give Him all of the praise and glory. Scott said it was such a blessing for him to experience. Not only to see Sydnee in a different angle, but also to hear people's responses. Scott said the thought crossed his mind that maybe this was a small taste of what Heaven will be like when we get there.

Also this week while Sydnee was at camp, she wanted to attend the big people's services instead of the children's church services. I don't really know why, other than she must have liked something about the adult services. One night, my mom called me to tell me that she had Mom to take her to the altar tonight at the close of the service. My mom agreed and took her down there. She said they prayed and after a few minutes, Sydnee raised her head up to look at her Nana and smiled and said, "I'm done." My mom told me she didn't really know what Sydnee wanted to pray about or what she said, but she really wanted to do it and was happy when she finished. I am thankful that Sydnee was sensitive to the Holy Spirit and that my mom was willing to let her go to the altar. God has a special way of reaching those who will listen.

Back at home after camp we were again preparing Sydnee for another surgery. This one, however, was going to be her last one for quite some time. When they had amputated her left foot in Boston, they left a screw in there to help hold the bones in place long enough for the bones to strengthen. They told us it would need to stay in there at least six months and then a short surgery could remove it. For this, we were able to stay local and just go to Knoxville. Her surgery would be outpatient and would not require her to spend the night. My mom was able to go with Sydnee, Noah, and me. Scott had to stay back to work and to be able to pick up Kerri from school.

Sydnee was a little nervous, but very excited at the same time to know this was the last one for a while. While in Knoxville, we were back at a familiar hospital where we knew several of the nurses, and more importantly, they knew Sydnee. Several of them commented on how much she had grown and how well she looked. Many of them hadn't seen her since she finished her chemotherapy almost two years earlier. It was another surgery and with that came the possibility that anything could happen, but through it all, yet again, there was a peace that this was the direction we should go. God was still guiding us and had His hand on her sweet little body. Sydnee came through the surgery very well and was so excited to get the opportunity to eat an orange Popsicle slushy afterwards. We were able to bring her home that evening, and she was ready to tell her Daddy and sister all about the events of our day.

Sydnee got back to normal and able to walk again following her surgery. Kerri was busy at school in the first grade, and Sydnee, Noah, and I were busy doing life each day. I tried to work on school work with Sydnee each morning. One morning in particular she just wasn't having it. She was guessing at what letters or shapes were and I knew that she knew many of them, but that she wasn't trying. We put the books away and then brought them back out a little later, and she was a little more cooperative. She was actually pretty ornery this time around. I would ask her what a letter was and she would think for a while and then look at me and ask, "Do you know what it is?"

I answered, "Yes."

She would then think some more and look back at me to say, "Are you going to tell me what it is?" and smiled so sweetly. How can you turn down someone so cute and headstrong at the same time?

The next day was Friday, August 27, 2010, and Sydnee was in a great mood. She was ready to do her schoolwork and get the day started. We practiced the letter "L." She loved it because she said it was easy to write and it looked like a checkmark. As we were cleaning up a little later, I asked her if she would practice writing her name because Grandparents Day was coming up and she would want to write her own name in the card. Now was a perfect time for her to practice. She agreed and wrote her name only once on the paper, but it was perfect! All big and messy, but all of the letters in the correct order and place. She was so proud! When Kerri came home from school that evening, she was so excited to show Kerri all of her homework from the day. After finishing Kerri's homework, the girls decided they wanted to play "school." Kerri was the teacher, Sydnee was the student named Kerri, and Noah and the baby dolls were the rest of the class. It was so cute. I tried to videotape them in "school," but I was told that wasn't allowed in the classroom by the teacher (Kerri). I was, however, allowed to take a few pictures of the three of them playing together.

Saturday was an unusual day for us in that we were going to be home this weekend without anywhere to be. It was fabulous! Scott was able to get some yard work done while I cleaned the inside of the house. The kids were so excited to have a pajama day and not have to get dressed to go somewhere. It was great to hear them play together and giggle at little things. Life was definitely good. That evening, we had made plans to go to our friends' house to eat dinner together. After dinner, the girls played with their kids while my friend and I tried to scrapbook some. It was a relaxed evening just like the whole day had been. Halfway through the evening, Sydnee came into the room where we were working and wanted to sit with us. She was very sweet and quiet and very happy to cut and glue papers together at the table with us. At the time, I thought it was a little odd for her to prefer sitting at the table with us than to play Barbies. Sydnee, however, had a fabulous time asking lots of questions and talking about nothing in particular. I guessed she just needed some Mommy time and found the perfect opportunity to get me to herself. I loved every minute of it!

We had survived almost five months of having three children in our house, and it was surprisingly peaceful. I was waiting for the other shoe to drop or for the chaos to begin at any moment. God, however, seemed to have His hand on our family, and we were making it. All of the children were happy, healthy, and loving life. God was so faithful and so close to us. It was a wonderful relaxing weekend and I was so thankful. I certainly wasn't taking these special moments for granted. I was aware of every one and thankful for them all.

Here am I, and the children the LORD *has given me.*
Isaiah 8:18

Chapter 14

THE DAY OUR LIVES CHANGED FOREVER

Sunday morning started out a little crazy because we had let the kids sleep in. The only problem was when we woke the girls up we had to start getting dressed and ready for church right away. Sydnee wasn't ready to get moving that quickly and was a little grumpy. We made it to Sunday School and church on time and Sydnee was still a little grumpy and clingy to us. Finally, she agreed to go to toddler's church with Miss Annah, and when we picked her up after service, she was fine. The grumpies were gone and everyone was happy.

After church, we ate lunch with some friends from church and went home. The day progressed as normal, and we were blissfully happy. We put the kids to bed at their normal bedtime and were just settling into our evening together on the couch. A friend of ours from church was staying in our basement for a few weeks during the week and then traveling to see his family on the weekends. He had just returned to our house and we were catching up on his weekend. Somewhere around 10:45 pm, Sydnee called out for Scott saying her leg was itching. This was a pretty normal occurrence since her de-bulking surgery in January on her right leg. Most nights, she would wake up once with her leg itching and Scott or I would go into their room and rub her leg until she would go back to sleep. We weren't sure if it was phantom pain or truly itching from the leg healing, but it occurred frequently and we were used to it.

This waking up itching went on every half-hour or so until we realized at 2:00 am that she had a temperature of 103.9. We were worried of course but tried to cool her off as best we could and even gave her some Motrin or the "big guns" as we called it. Since Motrin is excreted in the kidneys and Syd only had one kidney, we tried not to give her ibuprofen very often unless it was very necessary. She seemed to go right back to sleep, so we tried to as well. By 4:30 am, she woke up vomiting. We knew then we were probably facing a stomach virus. We braced ourselves for the "tsunami" this week because it was only a matter of time before the rest of us caught it.

We finally made it to the normal morning hours of 7:00 am, and we got Kerri dressed and ready for school. I felt bad for Kerri because I knew she hadn't slept much at all last night because they shared a room. Kerri was acting fine and ready to go to school, so we sent her. We called the doctor's office and they said they were seeing a stomach virus going around and that the high fever should go away in 8-10 hours, then other GI symptoms would begin. They said it was fine to keep her home and to treat the symptoms today. For whatever reason, it calmed my fears and I had a peaceful feeling about it. *So, it's a stomach virus,* I thought. *I can handle this.* My main concern was to quarantine Noah away from Sydnee so that he wouldn't get the virus. I was still breastfeeding him, so whenever I would go into Syd's room, I would use lots of hand sanitizer and change my shirt often.

As the morning progressed, Sydnee followed suit with what the nurse had said. The high fever was going away along with the vomiting. She was able to tolerate clear liquids and had eaten some Jell-O and "oval crackers" (Town House crackers). I had noticed as the afternoon was coming, she would ask to go to the potty and I would scoop her up and take her. While she sat on the potty, it was almost as if she would pass out for a brief moment. I would call her name and rouse her, but she wouldn't potty. When I got her back into bed, she was herself again, alert but tired. This happened a few times and by then Scott and Kerri were home. I had spoken to Scott about it earlier on the phone, but now that he was home, he saw it firsthand. It bothered both of us. The only thing we could come up with was that maybe her right leg, the big one, was pulling all of the fluid into it and making her orthostatic when she was upright. We feared that she was dehydrated and knew we had to do something. We decided Scott would take her into the after-hours clinic while I kept Noah and Kerri at home since I still had to feed Noah. We figured she would be admitted to the hospital for IV fluids for at least one night and then be released home. Scott grabbed a magazine while I changed Sydnee's gown and kissed her goodbye. She asked what was going to happen at the doctor's office. I told her as honest as I knew that she would probably have to get a straw in her arm (IV) and get some fluids and spend the night at the hospital. She seemed okay with that and didn't argue or question.

Scott left with Sydnee around 6:00 pm. He said he would call when they had her settled. I finished cleaning the kitchen and warmed up our friend's dinner who was staying with us. He had just gotten home from work, and I was telling him how Sydnee was going to the clinic when my phone went off. It was a text from Scott and it confused me. I read it again out loud and looked at our friend. I quickly dialed Scott's phone and asked him what was going on. He sounded panicked and said she was unresponsive and that they were calling the ambulance for her and that I needed to get down there quick. I must have looked scared because all I remember saying to our friend was that I had to go. I pulled frozen breast milk from the refrigerator and ran out the door. I don't remember telling Kerri anything and I felt bad about that, but I had to get there fast. The whole ride there, I prayed and prayed for Sydnee. I tried to call my friend Lori and ask her to pray. I left a message for my friend Cindy and prayed some more. I had told my friend to call our parents before I left the house, so I knew that was taken care of.

I got to the clinic as fast as I could and

found Scott running down the escalator steps and telling me they were bringing her out now. I turned around and saw about four people running with a gurney towards the ambulance, and then I saw her sweet little head. They had the ambu bag on her face and I asked the doctor if I could ride in the ambulance with her. She said no, so Scott and I loaded up in one car and followed the ambulance to the hospital. We parked and were out of the van by the time they were getting her out of the ambulance. We ran closely behind the crowd of workers and listened as they said she still had a pulse and her pupils were reactive to light.

We made it to the PICU and the nurse asked us if we wanted to wait outside. We wanted to stay with her, so we stood behind the workers near the head of the bed and watched everything. That small room filled with people and equipment so quickly. They tried to intubate her, but they couldn't get a tube to advance. Each time they would drop something on the floor, I was screaming inside, *Just pick it up, it doesn't matter about the germs. Just hurry!* All the while, Scott was busy texting people asking them to pray and crying. I was praying almost having a conversation with God Himself. I remember telling him that Sydnee was His child and we wanted His will to be done. We had committed her into His hands a long time ago when she was first born. Since then, we have trusted in His leading, His ways. Could this be His will? I knew He could make her wake up, to make everything okay if He so chose. At the same time, I also somehow knew we were losing her, but full of hope with everything in me that it wasn't true. It was a pleading kind of prayer that I hadn't ever prayed before.

The doctors and nurses were talking out loud to each other, and I knew what they were saying. I knew what it all meant. I watched the monitors, and then I would look back at my beautiful little girl's face willing her to open her eyes and get up. They said they couldn't feel any pulses peripherally on her arms or legs. I knew her body was shutting down. I watched as they tried to get an IV anywhere they could. I remember telling them not to use the right leg because of her syndrome. They checked her heart devices via ultrasound and they were intact and working. It didn't make any sense. They started CPR. I watched every squeezing of the ambu bag, every chest compression, and every dose of epinephrine. Scott said he remembers pulling me back ever so slightly as they announced they needed another person to take turns with compressions. I was a nurse, and I was ready to do what I had to do to save my daughter. It was there that the lines between being Sydnee's mother and a nurse blurred a little. They needed help and I knew how to help. They called for the red crash cart and for the paddles. I watched every shock of her little body with the paddles. Why wasn't this working? I remember counting the doses of epinephrine that they had given her. It was a lot and it should be working. Each time they would pause to see if it was taking effect, they would resume compressions again. There was no response and her sweet little body laid there lifeless.

They had worked on her for over an hour and a half and did everything they could to help her, but it didn't work. Finally, at 8:15 pm, they stopped everything and let her go. The doctors looked at us and said they were so sorry, but she was gone. The next few minutes are somewhat of a blur to me, but I remember the nurses, doctors, and technicians leave the room; it was just one nurse left and us. How quickly the room became almost empty. I quickly asked her if I could hold Sydnee, and she said yes. With her in my arms, Scott said the only words that came out of my mouth were, "Run Sydnee, run to Jesus! You're free! You have your skin legs now, sweet girl." It was so peaceful, yet so unreal at the same time. I don't know how it happened, but I know time seemed to stand still as I held my precious daughter. I remember combing her hair with my fingers and holding her tightly as Scott held the both of us.

At some point in all of this, my tears stopped flowing and I had something like a thought go across my mind. It was very clear, but quick, "It's not that bad!" It would take days for me to remember this, but it was there, and it was real, and I'll never forget that moment! In that moment, she was my sleeping Sydnee, and I so desperately wanted her to wake up and smile as though she were just pretending to be asleep. In that moment, I knew our lives were forever changed.

Peace I leave with you; My peace I give you. I do not give to you as the world gives. Do not let your hearts be troubled and do not be afraid.

John 14:27

Unbeknownst to me, our friend had gotten in contact with my parents and they had asked him to call some of our church friends to go to the hospital to be with us so that we wouldn't be alone. We evidently had a pretty large crowd of our church friends collected in the hallway. One of the associate pastors came into the room to be with us. It was such a great comfort to have people who cared so much for us. Scott made a few phone calls to let our families know. He called our house to check on Kerri and Noah and learned someone else from our church had come over to keep Noah while our friend had brought Kerri to the hospital. Scott went out into the waiting room to find Kerri and to talk with her. I couldn't leave Sydnee alone, so Scott went by himself. He said by this time, it was pretty crowded in the hallway, and Kerri hugged him when he found her.

Scott looked for a room to take Kerri to talk to tell her about Sydnee's passing. My friend Cindy was there by this time, and Scott asked her to go with them. Scott said that Kerri cried and hugged him so tightly when he told her. He said it was the hardest thing he had ever had to do. After a while, Scott wanted to come back into the PICU to check on me, so he asked Kerri if she wanted to go back to see Sydnee with him. She didn't want to, so she stayed with Cindy. During all of this Dr. Shook, the pediatrician, showed up to check on us. He was visibly upset and offered his condolences and sincerest apologies for not being there. I told him not to worry about it and that we didn't in any way expect him to be there. He offered to help me bathe Sydnee and get her cleaned up. He was truly a picture of a loving doctor who had been touched by my Sydnee.

We cleaned her up and brushed her hair. He helped me make handprints of Sydnee's hand and then helped me clip some of her hair to keep. I think I was still in shock over all of this, but I remember thinking how nice and yet how strange it was to be doing this. Our pediatrician is truly gifted in his care and treatment of children. Scott came back into the room as we were finishing up with Sydnee's handprints. He was as amazed as I was to see our pediatrician there with us at such a late hour. I will never forget his acts of kindness that night nor will I ever be able to repay him for all that he has done for our children.

Kerri finally decided she wanted to come into the PICU with us to see Sydnee. Scott went out to get her and she looked like she was scared to death when she walked into the room. I was sitting on the bed beside Sydnee, and I could tell Kerri wanted to hug me, but she was clinging very tightly to her daddy's hand. We talked to her a little about Sydnee and all on her own, Kerri said, "I knew she was going to die."

Scott asked her, "How did you know? We didn't even know."

She said, "Jesus told me." We were shocked and didn't know what to say about that. We let it go and moved on. We talked with Kerri about how our bodies are just a shell and when we die, our soul inside of us goes to Heaven with Jesus if He lives in our hearts. She thought about it a little while and then said, "Is it like an egg? A shell on the outside and our feelings are the good parts inside."

We said, "Yes!" Wow! Barely six years old, and that comes out of her mouth! Somehow, as basic as we could get it, she understood somewhat. Eventually, Kerri sat on the bed beside Sydnee, but she wouldn't touch her, and that was okay. I didn't want to shield her from this. To us, death is a normal process of life. She needed to see this and to know it was okay. She wanted to go back out into the waiting room where some toys were as well as some friends. Scott took her back out and people kept coming into Sydnee's room to check on us. My parents had arrived by this time and were able to see Sydnee one last time. She laid there with her left leg bent slightly like she always did. It was as though she was only sleeping.

After a while, Dr. Shook said we should probably limit the visitors because we still didn't know what had happened. He was thinking it was the bacteria that caused meningitis. It can hit rapidly and make someone sick pretty quickly. Because of this, we would have to be treated for prevention against it. I felt badly because some were able to come in and some now were not. We were just trying to be careful when we clearly didn't know what we were facing. Dr. Shook had written a prescription for Scott and me, but unfortunately, the 24-hour pharmacy was out of the liquid form for the kids. We would have to take them to the doctor's office tomorrow for a shot.

I could have stayed there holding my baby girl forever, but it was getting pretty late by now, and we knew the nurses needed to take Sydnee's body. After one last hug and kiss to Sydnee, we started to leave. I remember not feeling my legs move, but somehow, I was walking. When Sydnee was in the hospital for surgeries, I would never leave her for very long. I would go down the hallway to the restroom only when a favorite nurse was able to sit with her or a family member was available. How was I going to leave her now?

I remember walking out into the hallway and seeing friends and family there. Many had already left and gone home, but we gathered Kerri and her things and made it to the elevators. We walked out of the hospital hand in hand somewhere around 1:30 am.

The loneliness and confusion had now begun. I was tired, shocked, numb, and I physically hurt all at the same time. At home, our friend Shep met us on our driveway. He had evidently jumped into his car at the first call and had driven five hours to be with us. I was so glad to see him. Scott's parents had arrived shortly after that, and we were so tired after retelling the events of the day to everyone there at the house. Kerri was exhausted and ready for bed. It was close to 3:00 am when we finally went to bed and tried to sleep. I needed to be near my children, so all four of us slept in our bed together. I remember looking at Kerri and Noah while they slept and noticing the "hole" between them in the bed. It was for Sydnee, and she wasn't there.

Chapter 15

HARD DAYS AHEAD

The next few days were very long and very hard. Poor little Kerri cried a lot and asked a lot of questions. She was six years old, and I know she didn't understand all the hows and whys because at 31, I didn't understand them either. Even baby Noah, at five months old, was a little fussy and clingy to me. He must have picked up on our moods and the atmosphere around our house. After school, a few of Kerri's teachers as well as her school principal stopped by our house to check on us and to offer their condolences. We had several people drop off food, flowers, and to see if they could do anything for us. It is all a little bit of a blur. I know my house was full of people staying with us and some not. I just remember walking around my house watching everything. When it would get too much, I would look for Scott or just go upstairs to my bedroom. That seemed to be the one place where no one came and I could hear myself think. I am so thankful for all of the help with our house, the kids, and everything. It seemed like I was feeling alone and trying to connect with Scott to find the only other person who knew completely what I was feeling. It seemed like every time Scott and I had a free minute together, someone else would walk in the room with a question, phone call, or something else that needed our attention. At one point, I pulled Scott aside and told him that he was allowed to grieve in whatever way he needed, but to please not shut me out. We were the only ones here who knew how each other felt, and I needed him as much as he needed me.

All evening long, Kerri kept asking us when she could go back to school. I really didn't know how to answer her. How long is long enough for her to be gone? I hadn't experienced this before and it was new to us. I asked one of her teachers for advice. She thought it might be good for her to try going back to school when she was ready to get back into her "normal" routine. She said we could at least try it, and if it was too much for Kerri, then she could come home.

The next day, two days after losing Sydnee, Kerri went back to school. Both Scott and I walked her into her classroom and gave her a super-big hug before we left. When Kerri walked into her classroom, it was almost as if she was a celebrity amongst her friends. Her two best friends came right up to her and gave her big hugs and told her they missed her. As we walked out of the classroom, I saw a smile on Kerri's face and knew she would be okay. Her teacher smiled and winked at us with a look that said she would take care of her. That was exactly what my "mommy heart" needed at that present moment. I remember as we walked down the hallway from her classroom, several other parents simply looked at us. I know they didn't know what to say, and in all reality, they couldn't have said anything to help or make the hurt go away.

I just remember feeling so different. I was now one of those people who would have a sticker on my car that was "in loving memory" of a loved one.

After we left the school, Scott and I went driving around town to look at the cemeteries and try to get a few moments alone together to make some plans. Even though we had now lived in Kingsport for six and a half years, we still didn't know anything about the cemeteries or funeral homes. Why would we? We drove by the only cemetery that I knew of because it was on the way to the airport. We thought we would start there since we knew how to find it. We drove to the top of the hill where the funeral home was located and walked inside. Someone came to help us and in minutes, we were inside of a room talking with someone about the services they offered there.

From the moment we walked in the door, there was a peace. I really cannot describe it any differently. Just a feeling that we would be okay and that this was the place to put Sydnee. We had already told the hospital to send her to another funeral home in town, but they said they could take care of moving her for us if we so chose.

The funeral director wanted to know a little about my baby girl. Who she was, what she liked, and other things. We walked around with them and even looked at their mausoleums. It was there that we found the perfect spot for our little girl. It was a double vault, which was more than we needed, but it had the morning sun reflecting on the square and it was beside the window looking over a beautiful green pasture. I started to get a little teary and looked at Scott. He felt it too. This was the place. We later learned the row that she was going to be placed was called the heart level. She was a piece of our hearts. Every morning when she would wake up, she would say, "It's morning day! Time to get up!" This place would have the morning sun. Along with this, the spot beside her was available and would hold both Scott and me whenever we passed. If there could be a "perfect spot," this was it. We had made plans to have lunch with Kerri at school that day, so we couldn't stay long. We made plans to come back later that afternoon to make the final arrangements. We left there feeling like we were doing the right thing and once again, there was peace.

When we went back, we took both of our fathers as well as our pastor to help us plan the service and to write the obituary. Talk about rough. I was beginning to see that Scott and I grieve very differently. I knew there was a task at hand, and we needed to get through it. Scott, on the other hand, was lost. It was almost as if he couldn't complete a thought or make a decision. It was a little frustrating, but we made it through all of the tough decisions. We wrote her obituary together and chose a casket. They didn't have the one we wanted in the room, but they could order one in time. We chose a pink exterior casket with pink interior as well. It came with an inlay that had the word "princess" written in purple. It would be perfect for our little princess. We chose a marker that was named Sussex which was also the name of the street where we lived. The color of the stone had a pink tint to it when light shone on it. In reality, did it really matter that much to have all of those little details? Probably not. But to this hurting mommy's heart, it was a big deal. It was perfect for one of my treasures.

I had one other request. I remembered that when my older cousin died, her parents had her name written on her headstone in her own writing. Since this was Sydnee's latest accomplishment, I knew I wanted to at least try. I brought the paper with me and showed it to the planners. We copied it and I traced it in black marker. We faxed it to the company and they said they could do it. Since it was only her first name, we decided to add a second plaque with only her first name written in her own handwriting. I knew I also wanted to include her life verse on the marker. It was rather lengthy and it wouldn't fit in its entirety. We had to shorten it a little to make it fit in the allowed space.

You created my inmost being; You knit me together in my mother's womb. I praise You because I am fearfully and wonderfully made; Your works are wonderful, I know that full well. My frame was not hidden from You when I was made in the secret place, when I was woven together in the depths of the earth. Your eyes saw my unformed body; all the

*days ordained for me were written in Your book
before one of them came to be.*
                                        Psalm 139:13-16

It was now time for the payment of all of
this. The funeral home workers very delicately
handed us the paperwork to sign. Scott signed his
name and then I signed mine and then looked at
how much we would need to pay. At the bottom of
the paper, I saw the number that shocked me and
made my eyes tear up. I pointed to the total and
showed it to Scott. He looked at me and we knew.
The total for that portion of the funeral expenses
was $7574.00. I wouldn't have included this
information, but it is evidence to how our God
works. Remember back to the love offering that was
given to us for Sydnee's care? The total of the
offering was almost exactly the total of this bill
($7500.00). All along, we knew the money was hers
and just always felt like we should save it for her to
use down the road for something. Perhaps she
would want a new prosthesis that was for water or
something that insurance wouldn't cover. We had
struggled with accepting this money in the first
place. Along with this, we fretted over spending it
on her. Up until now, we had put it in the bank into
an account for her. It had given us a peace by doing
this. We wrote the check and sat there shocked at
what we had just seen. God was even here with us
in her death. He had a plan, and it was becoming
more evident what His plan for her life was.

As the week progressed, we had more and
more family members begin to show up. Scott and I

were very busy selecting pictures for my brother-in-law to use in a power point presentation of her life. We wanted to use songs that were special to us or her. We chose one of the songs from her "Sydnee" CD that used her name in the song several times. We also included the song we used for her baby dedication, a song from her "no more chemo" celebration, and a few others. One of our favorites was "Sisters," from the movie *White Christmas*. It just happened to be my favorite Christmas movie, and the girls had latched on to it as their favorite as well. It described our girls perfectly!

All in all, we went through over 8000 snapshots that we had taken of our family. It was very time-consuming, but it was an opportunity for Scott and me to relive Sydnee's life right there in pictures. We both remarked how no matter what she was going through there was a smile on her face. It was just another reminder that we were trusting God in this as well. He had carried us through so many rough times in her life, and even in her death He was still there carrying us. It seems very simplistic to say that, but it is so true. This was without a doubt, the hardest thing I ever had to do, and yet, I didn't have to do it alone. My husband and I took turns being distracted and busy with other people, but God was always there giving us each the strength to face another day. At the end of each day, He was letting us lay our heads down to bed and actually sleep. We rested and were making it. I remember waking up a lot, but I could just as easily fall back to sleep. It was a gift from God alone, and I was so thankful for even these little things.

Friday came finally and I went to the funeral home to polish Sydnee's fingernails and to fix her hair. I felt very strongly about this, and I wanted to do it one last time for my little girl. The workers at the funeral home were so gracious to allow me to do this. Scott, my mom, and my sister went with me to get her ready. We took a few pictures of each step of her life and I wouldn't miss this one. I know that sounds a little morbid, but I wanted it. Scott would hold one of Sydnee's hands while I polished her nails and then give that hand to my sister to hold while it dried. My mom helped take pictures and hold the curling iron or whatever I needed. It was a sweet few minutes, and I was so thankful to have had this opportunity. I needed it. We touched up her makeup a little and put the finishing touches on her clip-on earrings. She loved them and didn't look right without them. Before leaving, we asked the workers there if they could try to do a hand mold on Sydnee's hands for us. They agreed and let us do it.

It was around 3:00 pm when we received a phone call from Scott's office saying that the pathologist who performed the autopsy on Sydnee had called looking for Scott. He said the preliminary report was back and wanted to know if Scott would like to hear the results. We talked about the pros and cons of finding out right now only hours before the viewing. Finally, we decided it would be best and would perhaps help us make a little sense out of her death. Scott called the doctor back and talked with him for a while. After the phone call, he talked with me and said that everything looked okay and that there really wasn't anything abnormal for her. We sat there for a while and tried to process all of that. In the end, strangely, even though they couldn't find an exact cause as to why she died, it brought both of us such a huge peace. It was in that moment that we finally felt like as health care professionals and her parents, we hadn't missed anything. We had worried so much all week long about how we could have prevented this or what we could have done differently. In the end, we just had to accept that this was God's plan for her young life. It just felt like such a load was lifted. Don't get me wrong, it still hurt, and we were not happy that we had to lose Sydnee, but knowing that this was completely out of our hands and that we didn't miss anything, that we did exactly what we could and it still wasn't enough. Strangely, it became a comfort. My prayer was: "God, you know exactly what you are doing and we simply don't. Please help us to accept this as Your will for Sydnee's life. Help us to rely on You for the answers and for the comfort that only You can give." It was a complete surrender of Sydnee to Him and His perfect plan. It was the hardest thing we had ever faced, and yet at the same time, it was as if it was our only option and that brought peace.

Scott and I had requested that we have a few minutes alone with our "five family" before everyone else started to show up at the church for the visitation. It was a special ten minutes or so reflecting on special memories we had as a family. Of course, the mommy in me straightened her hair a little and put the finishing touches in her casket--her princess shoes. These shoes were such a big thing for Sydnee and she was so proud this summer as she was finally able to fit into a pair of plastic princess dress up shoes. She earned them and she was going to be buried with them. I placed them on the side of her casket and stood back to admire this precious sight. My baby girl dressed in pink as beautiful in death as she was in life. Along with her princess shoes, we also gave her special black and white stuffed Dalmation puppy named "Lucky" to her and her blanket. She had a special way of folding her blanket on the corner to fit just perfectly between her first finger and thumb. She then would touch it to her mouth to rub on her lips. Scott helped me fold the blanket just so and secure it in her hand one last time.

I scanned the church to see a plethora of pink flower arrangements all over the place. Sydnee would have squealed in delight to see so much pink! It was fabulous! Later on, one of the men in our church told us that he had heard that all of the flower shops were running out of pink flowers because of Sydnee's service.

As the evening progressed, we went to the church for the visitation and were able to greet people for over three hours. The line was so long and filled with so many people offering their condolences to us in our time of loss. There were so many faces of people I had never even met standing there in line just to say what an impact our little girl had on their life. Many of them had simply heard about her and had prayed for her at different times in her life. It was such a blessing to see that others could see what a miracle God had performed in her short life.

I was so afraid that people would misunderstand our calmness with relief that Sydnee was gone. Here we were facing our greatest fears as parents in losing our child, and we were okay. We weren't taking medicine to cope, we were sleeping somewhat, and we were making it. I told these concerns to our friends, Shep and Lori, and they both denied that people saw that in us. They said that by watching us all evening, they could see God's grace and peace evident in us. That's exactly what we felt. For now, it was a sense of: "Lord, I don't have to know all of the answers right now, I just know that You are here with me and You are sustaining my family today."

Saturday morning, the day of the funeral, Scott and I both woke up with a sense of dread. This was finally "the day" we had been dreading all week long. We had worked so hard going through pictures for a tribute of Sydnee's life as well as planning the service. Now it was time to prepare our hearts for telling our baby girl goodbye for the last time this side of heaven. I don't really think you can ever fully prepare for something like this, but it is almost a sense that this is the last thing we can do for her here on Earth. We had asked both of Sydnee's uncles to serve as pallbearers as well as my uncle (Syd's great uncle) and our good friend Shep. All four men were honored and humbled to be given such an honor. My dad, Sydnee's Poppy, would bring the message for the service. Our pastor would read the eulogy as well as offer some personal remarks and then Shep, our friend would say a few words. All of these men decided to wear pink neckties in honor of Sydnee, and I must say, it was a handsome group of men. Sydnee would have been so happy! We walked into the church and saw the men and women from the funeral home also wearing pink in honor of Sydnee. We didn't ask them to; they just did, and it was so thoughtful and a gesture we certainly will not forget. It was little things like this that we experienced all week long and throughout Sydnee's life that reminded us of God's grace and comfort. He hadn't forgotten us, and He was here with us today, sustaining us for the journey ahead.

The funeral was absolutely beautiful. I could have sat there all day long and listened to stories about Sydnee Danielle and the impact she had on so many people's lives. My brother-in-law sang several songs and did an amazing job under the circumstances. The Lord's anointing was definitely with my daddy as he spoke the "Poppy's princess message" that day. I was so worried about him being able to make it through this day. It had been a long week where I had seen my dad brought to tears on so many occasions. He would pull me aside from all of the chaos at my house and let me read what notes he had written at the time, and he would get choked up just going over this with me. How was he going to be able to do this? The same way we were all were, simply by the grace of God alone.

We tried to include as many "Sydnee-isms" as we could in the service. It just seemed to make it a little more customized to truly capture what a special little girl she was. At the end, we concluded with singing two of her favorite songs. The first one was "Holy, Holy, Holy" and the second was "Holy Ground" also known as the "angel song" to Sydnee. Looking back on it now, it amazes me that those songs would be so special to her. She loved them. Those were the 2 songs that we would catch her singing while she played around the house or she thought she was alone and no one was listening. There was such a spirit of God there with us it was almost like a celebration of her homecoming. I remember hearing several people say, "Amen" or "that's right" or something to that effect during these closing songs. It was a celebration that made us each feel as though God Himself had come down from Heaven and let us taste ever so slightly what Heaven will be like. People were getting blessed and were worshipping right there, in a funeral service for my four-year-old little girl. It was a sweet spirit and a special time to be there. Oh, how I wished God would pull back the veil and let me see my Sydnee running and playing in Heaven. But, for now, I just have to wait.

The rest of the afternoon was spent going to the mausoleum for the committal service and then back to our church for a wonderful meal. It had been such a long day and we were all so very exhausted. Kerri even fell asleep on our way home to our house. Sunday morning came, and we decided not to go to Sunday School, but we went for church. Kerri didn't want to wear any of the shoes that she owned with her dress that day, and it made for an even more stressful morning. She cried most of the car ride to the church. None of us really wanted to go and face everyone there, but we knew we would have to eventually. It was definitely an act of faith. We made it and walked in to be seated in time for church. Kerri was sad walking into Children's Church all alone, but she went and had a decent time. I think she was just missing her best buddy. They had always done everything together. Now, Kerri was on her own until Noah was able to walk, at least.

After church, we couldn't decide where to eat and knew we needed to get out of the house. It was getting crowded there, and we were all tired of eating there I think. I just wasn't up to being out in public any more that day. We drove home to change clothes and to decide. Kerri really wanted to go to a local buffet, so we decided to call everyone that was still in town to go along with us. The longer it took, the more out of control I was feeling. I told Scott I didn't feel like going, but he didn't want to leave me alone. Poor thing, he really didn't know what to do. Finally, after a few tears, I was able to convince everyone that I would be fine and that I just needed some space. They all went to lunch and I collapsed on Sydnee's bed.

I just laid there and fell apart. The tears came so hard and it felt so good to let it all go. I missed my Sydnee terribly, and I felt the closest to her now, on her bed. It was there that my world felt right again. Where things didn't make sense, but they didn't have to. Where I could be Kristi and not someone's mommy, wife, or whatever role I was needed to be. I was hurting, and that was okay. After the tears came stillness. It was so peaceful and comforting. It was just what I needed.

Chapter 16

OUR NEW NORMAL

Scott returned to work and Kerri had already gone back to school. It was time for Noah and me to also begin our "new normal" at home together. It was such a strange time for all of us. I was lost without Sydnee underfoot and needing me to help her do something. She had only had these new prostheses a few months now, so she was still a little clumsy walking around in them sometimes. Along with this, she still needed help dressing herself as well as just normal handling of a four-year-old. Noah was only five months old at the time, and he was still taking two naps a day which made for a long day waiting until it was time to pick up Kerri from school.

When my mom left, she had cleaned my house and helped with laundry as per her usual routine, so I didn't have as much housework to do starting off. The house was strangely quiet. I tried to fill the house with noise because it suddenly became so quiet. I remembered listening to praise and worship music a lot while Sydnee was going through chemotherapy to help with my mood. I knew I had to keep my mind occupied and on praise-worthy things. If I dwelt too long on what I was missing out on as a mommy without Sydnee, I wasn't much good.

I tried to think in terms of knowing that God had a plan and that taking Sydnee from us so soon had to be His plan. I had to learn to trust this with every part of my being both day and night. It quickly became a time of: "Lord, please help me to see past this and to look for Your will and Your way instead of my hurting or wanting my will."

I spent a lot of time visiting the mausoleum and spending time with Sydnee during this early time. For the first two weeks following her passing, I was there most days. It was such a strange place to be at times. When it just became too much and I was missing her so much, I would load up Noah in the car and off we would go. Sometimes, I would have a lot to talk about, and others I would be speechless. As a Christian, I knew she wasn't there, that she was safe with Jesus in Heaven. As a mommy, I had to do something for her. Buying flowers for her vase, vinyl clings for the marble wall, buying cards or writing a small note to her was my way of tucking her in or celebrating a special day with her. It may seem silly, but she was still and will always be my little girl. Just because she isn't physically here in my arms doesn't mean I can turn off my love for her.

About two weeks after Sydnee's passing, Noah and I returned to our weekly Bible study. It was so tough to go back and to face everyone without Sydnee, but because of Sydnee, I had to. She loved going to Bible study with me and made many friends there. She learned more about God and His promises. As a tribute to her, I took a deep breath and began walking into the class. It was a teary first morning back, but one that blessed my heart also as I saw firsthand how her death and life had impacted those wonderful women at Bible study. One of her former teachers just cried as she saw me, and I realized Noah would be in her class this year.

Of course, the song we sang that day was "Holy, Holy, Holy" one of Sydnee's favorite songs. It was tough to make it through, but I kept reminding myself that God had a plan and a purpose in all of this, and I just had to wait to figure it all out. It was the prayers of this group of women who kept me coming and sustained me throughout the year. How can I say thank you enough for all of their encouraging words and prayers for my family and our new normal? They are an amazing bunch of women.

Each day was a struggle in and of itself. I would do pretty well as long as I kept busy and kept my mind on looking for ways to praise and trust God in all of this. We were slowly creating a mental count of how many days we had been without Sydnee. Our lives were lived in lieu of this new timeframe. At first, it was as though our lives stood still every Monday night from 6:00 to 8:15 pm. We mentally re-lived the events of those few hours. It left us void and hurting. This was a busy time in our house finishing up dinner, bath time and finally bedtime. Usually the kids were in their beds by 8:00 pm each night, which left Scott and me to quietly watch the clock for what seemed like an eternity of fifteen minutes. Sydnee died at 8:15 pm on a Monday evening. Our new normal became this clock-watching for a long while. It really wasn't that we were consciously watching the clocks—it was just amazing that no matter where we were or what we were doing at the time, one of us would happen to look at the time, and it was 8:15 pm. It marked one more week without her in our lives. We kept this pattern of life of marking each week by every Monday night for quite a while. Slowly, it progressed from measuring weeks to months. The 30th day of every month was a rough, emotional day. I forget exactly how long it took to finally live our lives as "normal," but it seemed quite a long time before we could just enjoy each day and not look for the significance of each one.

Another major milestone in our lives was returning to some kind of routine for our family of four. Going out to eat at a restaurant was a biggie for me personally. I still remember the first time we went out for dinner. The hostess asked me how many was in our party, and I just froze inside. I told her four, but felt as if I were betraying Sydnee or her existence in our lives. It may seem very irrational to think like that, but we were and always would be a family of five, just not in the eyes of the public. It was amazing to me that such a small thing would leave such a big impact on me.

A little while after this, we went to eat with some friends from church one Sunday. We needed to change Noah's diaper before we left the church, so we asked our friends to go ahead to get a table at the restaurant and we would be there soon. Once we arrived, we only had to wait about five minutes or so until our table was ready. The waitress called our name, and we were escorted to our table. At the table, the waitress asked if we minded to put a chair on the end of the table or we could split up our party into two tables. Scott and I looked at each other puzzled because by our count, we didn't need an extra chair. Then, it hit us that our friends were including Sydnee in their count. This time, however, it didn't bother me so much as it touched me. They remembered Sydnee as part of our family, even if it was done accidently. My friend was embarrassed at her mistake, but it touched me.

Kerri had been used to sharing a bedroom with Sydnee for about eight months now and she was very lonely without Sydnee around. Nighttime was the worst time for her. We caved every night and agreed to let her sleep in our bed. She stayed in our room for one month following Sydnee's passing. I think she was afraid of being all alone in her bedroom. Finally, we were able to convince her to sleep in her own bed and in her own room by herself. We prayed that God would give her a vision of Sydnee.

How desperately I wanted to see Sydnee and to see that she was okay. This time, however, my prayers turned to Kerri. I knew how desperately I wanted to see with my very own eyes my baby girl one more time. To see that she was okay and not to just believe. As close as Kerri and Sydnee were, I knew that my first princess, Kerri was hurting and full of questions. She needed this more than me now, I would just have to wait. I prayed that God would let her dream of Sydnee or of a great memory we had together. Just something small that would comfort Kerri and give her the hope that she would one day see Sydnee again. It wasn't something I would ever ask her about, but the mommy part of me so desperately needed to help my other daughter see.

Soon Kerri woke up one morning for school and bounded into our room. She was in such a good mood and laughing as she told us she had a dream about Sydnee. She said she saw a movie on the ceiling of her room. She said Sydnee had wings and was flying around their room, but she wasn't very good at it. She giggled as she told us all about it. She said Sydnee kept bumping into the walls and would laugh and say, "Oops!" It was a special treat for us to hear my big girl laugh in such an uninhibited way. It was a good start to a day and for this I was so very thankful.

Before Sydnee died, we had been planning a family trip to Walt Disney World in the fall during Kerri's fall break from school. The weeks following Sydnee's death, we weren't sure what we should do about the trip. Should we cancel or continue to go along as planned? Both Scott and I were thinking about cancelling the trip because our hearts just weren't into it. We simply were not ready to celebrate or to be happy just yet. How could we? We had just lost one of our treasures. Kerri overheard us talking and said she still wanted to go to Disney. She was upset to think that we couldn't go now. After bed that evening, Scott and I both knew that somehow we had to keep our initial plans to go to Disney. If for no one else for Kerri. She needed this and as her parents, we were going to do our best to get her there.

About six weeks after Sydnee's passing, we loaded up in an airplane and flew to Orlando, Florida—Disney bound. It was a struggle for both Scott and me, but we were determined to make sure Kerri had a wonderful time. Even though we didn't perhaps realize it at the time, we needed this as a family. To learn to celebrate every day! After all, it's the only one we have.

The trip was great. It kept us busy and gave us plenty of time to be with Kerri and Noah in a place that was geared to them. I must admit, walking into the "happiest place on earth" for the first time this trip was a little overwhelming and difficult. There is nothing like seeing Disney World through the eyes of your children. It becomes a magical place. A place where dreams come true. I missed my Sydnee so desperately. She was such a girly girl and a princess. She loved everything Disney princess with Cinderella being her favorite princess of all time. Being there made us miss her even more. My greatest desire was to see my Sydnee again. Just to know that she was okay. To see her with my very own eyes that she was whole again, complete, and not lacking anything. For now, I just have to wait.

We had made special t-shirts to wear during this trip for both of the girls—one was light blue with purple lettering that said Kerri's Day. The other one was light pink with hot pink lettering that said Sydnee's Day. We all wore the shirts for the girls and were amazed at the response. Kerri's Day was first and no matter where we were in the parks or hotel, people wanted to know who Kerri was and if it was her birthday. It even got us to the front of a line for a ride! Kerri beamed from ear to ear all day long because people wanted to know about her. Even though this happened to us for Kerri's Day, we just didn't think about it before we wore Sydnee's shirts. We were all dressed in our pink shirts, and again everywhere we went, people wanted to know which one was Sydnee. It presented us with a difficult task of telling a shortened version of her story to strangers, but at the same time, a wonderful opportunity to share a little about one of our greatest joys. Sure, it was difficult and most of the time, it brought tears to our eyes. However, it was important to share her story and to let others know that we were okay. God was so good to us. He was sustaining us and giving us strength for this day and so many others.

During one of the parades, one of the people in the grand marshall's car yelled out, "Yeah, Sydnee!" while waving to us. There was absolutely no way that lady could have known Sydnee was no longer with us. I'm sure she thought Kerri was Sydnee and today was her birthday or something. It captured my heart in that short moment and presented me with a choice. I could continue to be Sydnee's cheerleader, the role I had played for over four years now, or I could grow bitter and sad. I didn't want my kids to grow up in a home where their mommy changed when their sister died. Sydnee's death already marked a huge place in our lives that was now forever changed.

As their mommy, I'm supposed to help set the example. In that moment, something welled up within me and warmed my heart. Perhaps it was pride, or maybe just me pulling on my "big girl panties." I was so thankful for all of the days that I was blessed to be Sydnee's mommy. Living without her is certainly most difficult, and I don't understand it completely, but I want to use this in a positive way.

I don't have to worry about her anymore. She is okay. As a Christian parent, our biggest concern or wish for our children was that they would come to know, love and serve God with all of their hearts. To do this so that one day, when their lives on Earth are over, they may dwell in the house of the Lord, Heaven forever. This was just that! My Sydnee made it! It was so much sooner than I ever thought it would be, but just the same, she was okay. She was with the greatest parent there ever will be, her Heavenly Father.

Having said that, I am still human and wish selfishly at times she was still here with me. Of course, I was still sad and missing my precious daughter, but that day in Disney World, I was wearing her name so proudly and right over my heart. My perspective just changed a little more that day. It was more important to remember her laughter and imagine how much fun she would be having here with us today. My perspective changed in that split moment from some silly words from someone I'm sure I'll never meet. Why not choose to "celebrate everyday" as the parade theme suggested? My prayer from that day forward became: "Lord, please help me to be a good steward of her story. May others see You and Your love shining through even the darkest places."

We have this treasure in jars of clay to show that this all-surpassing power is from God and not from us.

2 Corinthians 4:7

Someone once told me that we don't have to have it all together all of the time. We can sometimes just be cracked pots because of the issues that we are facing or due to what we have gone through in our lives. It is in those moments that we are to let others see Christ shining through the cracks. His love and glory are in us, and He can shine in situations that seem so dark and hopeless.

The first holidays or vacations without your loved one are very tough to maneuver through, but we made it. Our traditions now included a trip to the cemetery. Such a strange tradition for us, but a much-needed one and one that we will continue for the rest of our lives. Our first Thanksgiving without Sydnee came just a few short months after her passing. I had to look a little harder for new reasons to be thankful. The hole in my heart from missing Sydnee was so deep, but God had been so gracious to us since her passing. It was as though we were being carried especially close to His heart during those times. Neither Scott nor I was truly in the mood to celebrate and be happy like normal. But we knew Kerri and Noah deserved and needed us to continue these traditions as we always did when we still had Sydnee with us. I wasn't fully committed to it, but my heart was searching for the peace that only God can bring. It was almost as if I was dreading the holidays coming and having to fake it because I certainly wasn't up to facing them. I clung to the verse in Psalms where it said that God knew all about me and that He was there for me. I needed more reassurance and comforting to face this new event. It was a strange place for me to remember Sydnee and to also make Thanksgiving fun, normal, and exciting for Kerri and Noah. It was this fear that seemed to grip my heart and cause the dread.

You have searched me, LORD, and you know me. You know when I sit and when I rise; You perceive my thoughts from afar. You discern my going out and my lying down; You are familiar with all my ways. Before a word is on my tongue You, LORD, know it completely. You hem me in behind and before, and You lay Your hand upon me. Such knowledge is too wonderful for me, too lofty for me to attain. Where can I go from Your Spirit? Where can I flee from Your presence? If I go up to the heavens, You are there; if I make my bed in the depths, You are there. If I rise on the wings of the dawn, if I settle on the far side of the sea, even there Your hand will guide me, Your right hand will hold me fast.

Psalm 139:1-10

The holidays came and went, and we made it. Yes, there were several hard days. I would find myself out Christmas shopping for my children, and I would actually put extra gifts in my cart for Sydnee without thinking. I was, in my mind, still shopping for three children. It really broke my heart when I realized what I was doing and had to put the gifts for Sydnee back on the shelf. Typically, I will buy gifts for my children throughout the year and save them for their birthdays or Christmas. I found gifts that I had bought early for Sydnee and didn't know what to do with them. It was too late to return them to the store. It seemed no matter where I went or what I was doing, there was always a constant reminder of the special place that was now void without Sydnee present.

Sometimes, I would cry because I didn't know what else to do. Other times, I would pray and ask the Lord to help me deal with all this sorrow and emptiness. It was in those times of total surrender to God's leading and direction that I would find peace and comfort that only He can provide. While it didn't always take the hurt away, it did, however, give me strength for the moment. That was exactly what I needed the most. To know that I would have to walk this road in my life, but that I certainly didn't have to walk it alone.

Chapter 17

MY LESSON

Very truly I tell you, you will weep and mourn while the world rejoices. You will grieve, but your grief will turn to joy.

John 16:20

While I cannot really say that I am joyful over losing my daughter, I can say, however, that the Lord has been so close to me in the days since. It is because of this closeness that my heart is turning to joy. This joy that is developing more and more in my heart is not a happy or giddy joy. It is a deep, settled, surrendered peace that God is in control and that He knows what is best. I will never "get over" losing my daughter, but I can get through this loss and turn it into something good with God's help. I am choosing to trust God and His plan in this. To change my perspective from what I am missing out on by not having Sydnee here to raise to the fact that I don't have to worry about her anymore. I know where she is, and she is safe and happy and perfectly content.

It took a while for me to get past the part about her being okay without her mommy with her. As a parent, it was my job to kiss away the pain from a boo-boo to make everything better. For Sydnee, Kerri or Noah I can't always take the hurt away. I can love them with everything that I have, but sometimes they are going to fall and get hurt. That scrape still hurts whether I am there or not. I can treat the surface with cleaning out the scrape, applying ointment, and then a band aid, but I have to let it heal on its own over time. That's just how this deep hurt is. True faith exists when we allow God to heal the hurt from the inside out. He comes so close to us that at times, it feels like we are being carried through the pain. Other times, we feel the full impact and the burn of the hurt or loss. It is in those times that we feel His peace and comfort that He is with us.

I have to take it day by day. One day is a good day or even part of a good day, another day can be a rough one. I am learning to praise Him for the good days and to draw close to Him through prayer and His word to lead me through the not-so-good days. Along with this, I am also confident that I am never alone. He is always there with me, leading me, guiding me and protecting me along the way. I simply have to allow Him to work in His will, His way, and His timing.

Early on after her passing, the night times were the hardest on me. I wasn't able to tuck Sydnee in and pray with her at night. To participate in family hugs with her before bed. It's sometimes the little things I miss so much. When I stop and think of where she is and that she is being taught by the Lord, it seems to make it all better.

All your children will be taught by the LORD, and great will be their peace.
                                                        Isaiah 54:13

I had to come to the realization that God could use my pain for my good and for His glory if I trust Him to work everything out. Yes, I was hurting and I was so sad and full of "why" questions, but deep down, I knew there could be a greater purpose in all of this. I still don't know exactly why He chose to take my daughter away from me, but I am trusting that He knows. I am learning that God always has His purpose in trials. One is that He gets the glory and the other is that He gives overflowing comfort to us so that we can help others.

Praise be to the God and Father of our Lord Jesus Christ, the Father of compassion and the God of all comfort, Who comforts us in all our troubles, so that we can comfort those in any trouble with the comfort we ourselves receive from God. For just as we share abundantly in the sufferings of Christ, so also our comfort abounds through Christ.
                                                        2 Corinthians 1:3-5

Kerri told us several times over the course of a year, "I knew that Sydnee was going to die. Jesus told me that she would get sick and that she was going to die and that we would be okay." Two summers after Sydnee's passing while we were on our vacation at the beach, Scott and I were sitting in chairs watching Kerri and Noah play in the ocean. They were laughing and having a great time jumping over the waves. Scott looked at me and said, "I guess this is what 'being okay' looks like." He was right. We are making it. We are okay.

May He receive all the glory, and may I know His joy!

Sydnee Danielle Coen
July 2, 2006 – August 30, 2010

UNSPEAKABLE JOY

REFERENCES

Cowman, L.B. "February 8." *Streams in the Desert: 366 Daily Devotional Readings.* Grand Rapids, MI: Zondervan Publishing House, 1997. 65-66. Print.

Holy Bible New International Version, Lavender, Reference Bible. Zondervan Publishing House, 2011. Print.

Made in the USA
Charleston, SC
15 May 2015